A Very Small Corner of
Paradise

This book is dedicated to

The memory of my parents
And to my husband
Our sons and daughter
Our grandchildren
And to all who have known and loved
This precious place

A Very Small Corner of
Paradise

The Story of Llanllŷr: a Garden in Wales

Loveday Lewes Gee

First impression: 2010

First published in 2010 by Y Lolfa in association with the
Ceredigion Branch of the Welsh Historic Gardens Trust

Editor: Penny David
Cover design: Alan Thomas
Cover photographs: Charles Hawes

ISBN: 978 184771259 2
Published, printed and bound in Wales
by Y Lolfa Cyf., Talybont, Ceredigion SY24 5HE
website www.ylolfa.com
e-mail ylolfa@ylolfa.com
tel 01970 832 304
fax 832 782

Paradise: A place or state of complete happiness.
The Garden of Eden in the biblical account of Creation.

The Greek writer, Xenophon (c.430–354 BC) described
the parks of the kings and nobles of Persia (Iran) that he
had seen in his travels. He uses the Greek word of Persian
origin, *paradeisos*, to describe these royal gardens that were
. vast enclosures that included fruit and ornamental trees,
flowers, birds and mammals.

'As so often in Wales, political reconstruction
and cultural renaissance went hand in hand.'

ACKNOWLEDGEMENTS

First of all I wish to thank Penny David. I owe her an immense debt of gratitude for her very considerable help and advice. Her encouragement and assistance have been absolutely invaluable.

I am also grateful to the Welsh Historic Garden Trust Ceredigion Branch for their support.

My thanks are also due to Charles Hawes for his photographs on the covers of this book.

The genealogies are based on research done by the late Major Francis Jones, formerly Wales Herald of Arms Extraordinary.

CONTENTS

INTRODUCTION

THIS IS THE STORY of a place and a garden. The place is called Llanllŷr and is to be found in a remote green and fertile valley near the west coast of Wales where the river Aeron makes its way towards the sea. This part of Wales is separated from the rest of the country by the Cambrian Mountains and this geographical isolation has nurtured an independence of spirit and self-sufficiency. Tradition is important although the origin of many of the rituals and the reasons for them have been long lost. Kindness and helpfulness to neighbours is a beneficial and rewarding element in this tradition, as is the emphasis on kinship and community. On the downside there is a certain disregard for an understanding of time and a lack of comprehension of any sense of urgency!

Llanllŷr has a long history encompassing Celtic Christian saints, Cistercian nuns, Tudor squires, Victorian gentry and, today, farmers and entrepreneurs. The story of this place is also the story of the gardens there. In the earliest times growing plants for food and medicine no doubt had priority, but pleasure gardens become increasingly evident as time progresses. The story is true insofar as certain historical facts provide the scaffolding to support the narrative, although a degree of supposition and imagination has proved necessary to fill the gaps, particularly in the earlier centuries. As far as the garden today is concerned the thoughts, eyes and memories of those who are or have been involved in its renewal provide the evidence.

The four chapters, related to the four seasons, are intended as metaphors for the four principal periods of garden-making at Llanllŷr. Winter evokes the slow awakening of nature at the beginning of the year, paralleling the coming of Christianity to Wales. Spring refers to the renaissance after the dissolution of the nunnery in the sixteenth century. Summer describes the prosperity and maturity of the Victorian era. Autumn explains the creation of the present garden by relating the various stages of development to the seven days of the week and to the days of Creation in the Book of Genesis.

During the restoration and development of the garden as it is today, the interests of the owners have found an echo in the various phases in the history of Llanllŷr. My own interest in the art of the Middle Ages is reflected in the symbolism of the Labyrinth and in the paving on the Stage. A love of Italy and a knowledge of Italian Renaissance gardens is suggested in the Water Garden and in the Box Garden near the house. The nineteenth-century layout survives and the contemporary planting complements the historic rose collection in the long borders.

It is perhaps presumptuous to refer to one's own place as a small corner of paradise but for those associated with it, it is just that. There are, no doubt, many others who would feel the same about their particular plot. Those who are fortunate enough to be enfolded in the bounteousness of a kind and beneficent nature are constantly aware of the wonders of Creation which surround us. Surely this is as close to Paradise as is possible on earth. All is not perfect, of course; pests and diseases, pernicious weeds, an unpredictable climate and many other hazards provide the challenges necessary to prevent complacency. Nevertheless, this story encompasses one and a half millennia when people have chosen to live and garden in this place – their own particular corner of Paradise.

CHAPTER 1

Winter:
Once Upon a Time

THE FIRST DAYS OF the year bring hope after the dark days of December. Just after the winter solstice the days start to get longer, imperceptibly at first, but one knows that improvement is on the way. The first day of the year is often bright, though rarely sunny, which emphasises the feeling of hope and renewal. At the start of the new year one begins to keep an eager eye open for the first flowers that confirm the renewal and rebirth. Initially just the first hint of colour, slowly spreading and growing in tune with the lengthening days, like the highlights of a quiet violin playing softly as the music of the orchestra slowly develops in the background building up for a climax later.

February is a transitional month, still slow and often inactive, often violent, cold and wet. Everything seems to be on hold for a period. Despite the adverse weather the emerging shoots of the native daffodil (*Narcissus pseudonarcissus*) keep hope warm in the heart. Much like a sprinter waiting at the blocks for the real start of the race. At the beginning of March the starting gun goes off. The sprinters shoot away and the golden flowers of the daffodils dance with their companions, the lowly pale yellow primroses (*Primula vulgaris*) and white wood anemones (*Anemone nemorosa*). Meanwhile the middle- and long-distance runners start their slow build up, gaining speed

Snowdrops are the earliest sign of the coming of spring and herald the re-awakening of the garden after the winter. These snowdrops are in the woods adjoining the Renaissance house and garden of the Lloyd family and would have been planted in the early seventeenth century. The first mention of snowdrops in Britain occurred in Gerard's *Herbal* of 1597.

and momentum to demonstrate their riches later in the year. Renewal has begun in earnest.

With hindsight one could imagine that a similar perception might be applied to the start of the first millennium after the birth of Christ. In many ways the pattern of the year, and the changes in the garden, mirror the changes over the last two millennia both in the wider aspects of history and in the story of Llanllŷr. In the first five hundred years, or the first three months, we see the slow spreading of the Word with highlights here and there. Life and hope grew and spread culminating in the bringing of Christianity first to Wales and shortly after to England. At Llanllŷr the possible founding of a shrine to a Celtic Christian saint may have preceded the establishment of the nunnery in about 1180.

The earliest written references to Llanllŷi
writings of Gerald of Wales of about 1190 to 12(
lists of Gervase of Canterbury of circa 1200 to
both refer to the nunnery for Cistercian nuns ......u by
Lord Rhys of Dinefwr, but the name suggests that there was
very probably an earlier Celtic foundation here. The word
'llan' denotes a church, chapel or enclosure, and such place
names are mostly of Celtic origin and are usually associated
with a dedication to a saint, in this case a saint called Llŷr. A
search through the lists of British saints reveals two possible
candidates.

Llŷr Forwyn, also known as Llŷr the Virgin, is one
suggestion, but nothing is known about her except that her
feast was on 21 October, the same day as that of St Ursula,
reputed to be the daughter of a British king. According to
a fourth-century inscription referring to the restoration of
a church in her memory, Ursula was martyred in Cologne
together with her companions. Her legend tells us that she
was a Christian who agreed to marry the son of a German
king provided he converted to Christianity and was baptised.
He agreed and Ursula set forth for Cologne with ten noble
female virgin companions. By the time that *The Golden
Legend*, featuring many saints' lives, was written in 1260 by
Jacobus de Voragine, a scholarly friar and Bishop of Genoa,
the number of virgin companions had grown to eleven
thousand. At Cologne they were all massacred by invading
pagan tribes of Huns. The thought that Llanllŷr might indeed
commemorate one of these martyred Christian virgins seems
appropriate, particularly as the site was later to be occupied
for more than three hundred years by holy nuns.

Llŷr, however, is normally a man's name and another
suggestion is Llŷr Merini, about whom little is known apart
from his inclusion in a list of Welsh saints, which includes
his genealogy. The name 'Merini' suggests that he may have
had some association with the sea from the Latin 'marinus'

eaning 'of the sea'. In Welsh legend Llŷr was the God of the sea.

Sanctity was locally conferred and saints' cults in Wales had an overwhelmingly local character, so it is possible that many churches with Celtic dedications in Wales are on the sites of small religious communities that were originally established by the saint whose name they bear or by one of his or her followers. Hermits and recluses, men and women, chose solitary sites and sought self-sufficiency, so hermitages were likely to have gardens adjacent to them. A seventh-century Celtic hermit, Manchan of Liath, described his ideal garden as 'Facing the south for warmth, a little stream across its enclosure, a choice ground with abundant bounties which would be good for every plant.' He could have been describing just such conditions that a hermit at Llanllŷr might have found.

Can we imagine how the hermitage may have been set out? Llanllŷr was situated on marginally higher ground protected on the north side by the river Aeron and on the west, south and east by marshes, in a fertile valley. It was solitary but at the same time accessible, since it is close to a river and near a roadway. The road crossing the river Aeron here connects major north-south and east-west routes. The village on the other side of the crossing is called Talsarn. 'Tal' translates as the end and 'sarn' indicates a paved road or causeway, such as Sarn Elen further to the east, connecting the Roman forts at Llanio and Trawscoed. According to legend this important road was named by the Roman Emperor Magnus Maximus (in Wales known as Macsen Wledig) for his Welsh wife, Helen. Folk memory suggests that the paved part of the road ended at the village and was apparent until a hundred years or so ago. Fragments of a stone cobbled road are still visible in places.

The ground here is peat marsh above a clay subsoil, surrounded by fertile, alluvial meadows. In former times woods may have extended over much of the valley. Oak trees grow particularly prolifically here. The hermitage may have been in a clearing in the woods and protected by marsh. The garden would have provided grain, vegetables, fruit and herbs, but possibly also some flowers to decorate the altar. The Romans brought vines to Britain but would the hermit here have had vines then? Vines are grown in the valley, today providing an excellent white wine when the weather is kind. Apples, pears, crab apples, sloes and other fruits would have been available to supplement the hermit's diet, as well as various wild offerings such as young nettles and ramsons or wild garlic in the spring and mushrooms and berries in the autumn.

Further evidence of the association of early Christians with Llanllŷr is an inscribed stone, split in half, which was found in the farmyard in 1859 and moved to its present position in the garden, where it now provides a focal point at the end of one of the paths. The stone, which experts have variously dated from the sixth to the ninth centuries, records the gift of a piece of land. A recent reading of the inscription:

TESQUITUS DITOC

QUA DOMNUACO

LLON FILIUS ASA

ITGEN DEDI[T]

has been translated as 'The hermitage of Ditoc [which] Occon, son of Asaitgen gave to Madomnuac.' The names are Irish, reflecting the extensive presence of the Irish in south-west Wales in the centuries following the departure of the Romans.

The only one of these names for which a possible identification has been suggested is Madomnuac, an Irishman who came to Wales to study under St David at his monastery

The Celtic inscribed stone records the gift of a piece of land to the Irish St Madomnuac, a disciple of St David at his monastery in Pembrokeshire, where he cared for the bees.

at Mynyw (now St David's) in south-west Pembrokeshire. The story of Madomnuac is included in Rhygyfarch's *Life of St David*. Rhygyfarch, who died in 1099, was born at Llanbadarn Fawr, near Aberystwyth, one of the sons of Sulien, Bishop of St David's, so the *Life* was written several centuries after the death of the saint, at a time when cultural and political priorities were very different. Nevertheless, the legend of Madomnuac (also known as Madomnoc, Domnoc, Dominic) as he tells it is of interest. Madomnuac was responsible for the bees at the monastery and looked after them with great care. When the time came for Madomnuac to embark on the boat to return to Ireland the bees followed him and settled themselves with him on the boat. He did not want to deprive the monastery of their bees so the boat returned to shore and the bees flew back to their hives. The same thing happened the next time Madomnuac set sail for Ireland. On the third occasion St David gave him permission to take the bees with him, blessing them before they left.

Any relationship or connection between St Llŷr, Ditoc's hermitage and Madomnoc has been long lost. Perhaps a hermitage originally founded by or in honour of Llŷr was later occupied by a hermit named Ditoc. Perhaps a further gift of land by Occon son of Asaitgen in honour of Madomnuac enabled the establishment of a monastery or hermitage with several hermits or recluses living in individual huts and sharing a church or oratory. Madomnuac was descended from the Irish royal line of O'Neil and is commemorated in various calendars on 13 February as a bishop and confessor.

Whether Llŷr or the Irish Madomnuac actually lived and gardened here we cannot now know but it is at least likely that associates or followers may have done so. It is indisputable, however, that from the late twelfth century nuns were established at Llanllŷr for three and a half centuries, and that some nunneries were founded on sites where religious people who had chosen to live apart from the world were already established. In the twelfth century an eremitic life was considered unsuitable for women, and groups of females who had gathered together to follow a religious life were regularised into nunneries. One example of this was the establishment in 1145 in Hertfordshire of a priory for the recluse Christina of Markyate and her followers.

The convent for Cistercian nuns was founded at Llanllŷr in about 1180 by the Lord Rhys ap Gruffydd of Dinefwr, Prince of Deheubarth, who placed it under the supervision of the Abbot of Strata Florida. This was an important Cistercian monastery about thirteen miles further inland, for which the Lord Rhys had provided substantial endowments and had greatly enlarged the lands and influence.

The establishment of the nunnery at Llanllŷr is interesting in that it is some forty years earlier than the first nunnery in England to be recognised by the Cistercian order. This was at Tarrant in Dorset by Bishop Richard Poore of Salisbury, before his translation to Durham in 1228, with the support of King Henry III and his queen, Eleanor of Provence, under whose patronage the Bishop placed his foundation. The king's sister, Joan, Queen of Scotland, chose to be buried there in 1238. Such influential sponsors explain the establishment of this nunnery. The only other nunnery in England accepted by the General Chapter of the Cistercians was at Marham in Norfolk, founded by another wealthy and influential patron, Isabelle de Warenne, Countess of Arundel, and consecrated in 1249.

The Cistercian order had been founded in 1098 at Cîteaux, in Burgundy, when a group of Benedictine monks, under their abbot Robert, wished to forego the luxury enjoyed by many rich monasteries and to seek a simpler, more austere form of religious life. The later charismatic leader St Bernard of Clairvaux (1090–1153) inspired the rapid spread of this movement across Europe. The Cistercians were, however, generally unenthusiastic about accepting women into the order, although women evidently found the austerity and spirituality very appealing. A number of nunneries claimed to be following the Cistercian rule, but only a very few were accepted by the General Chapter of the Order. One problem was the difficulty of finding an abbot to supervise the nuns. The Abbot of Strata Florida had already received many gifts from the Lord Rhys and was perhaps promised more if he agreed to do as his Patron wished. In fact the lands that the Lord Rhys gave to Llanllŷr were also generous, but a substantial part of these, according to Gerald of Wales, appear to have been acquired by Strata Florida.

It appears possible that the Lord Rhys may have founded Llanllŷr as a retreat for his female relatives. His sister Gwladus had been widowed as a result of the bloody feuds between the Welsh and the Norman Marcher Lords. Henry, Earl of Hereford, was slain in Gwent by Gwladus's second husband, Seisyll ap Dyfnwal, Lord of Upper Gwent, in 1175. Henry had no sons and William de Briouze inherited the Lordship of Brecon through his mother Berthe, one of Henry's three sisters. The *Chronicle of the Princes* described how in 1175 William took revenge for his uncle's death by luring the leading Welshmen of Gwent to his castle at Abergavenny where, according to the *Chronicle*, 'Seisyll ap Dyfnwal was slain through the treachery of the Lord of Brycheiniog [Brecon], and along with him Gruffydd, his son, and many of the chieftains of Gwent. And then the French fell upon the court of Seisyll ap Dyfnwal; and after Gwladus, his wife, had been seized, they slew Cadwaladr, his son.' Cadwaladr was aged seven and was, it seems, killed in his mother's arms.

There is a suggestion that Gwladus may have retired to Strata Florida after the deaths of her husband and two sons, very understandably seeking safety and peace after such a traumatic experience. Benedictine and Cistercian monasteries provided refuge and hospitality to travellers and pilgrims at guesthouses. At Cistercian abbeys such guesthouses were set apart from the main complex and there is evidence of this arrangement at Tintern Abbey. There are several instances in the records of abbeys in south Wales of complaints about the expense of providing hospitality for travellers. In the case of Strata Florida, the Abbot's agreement to supervise the nuns at Llanllŷr may have been encouraged by self-interest, not only on account of the cost of having as indefinite guests such an important noblewoman and her entourage, but also relief at the distance being placed between the ladies and his monks. When Llanllŷr was founded there were apparently sixteen nuns, many of noble birth.

Gerald of Wales commented that the nuns followed from the outset, as far as permissible, both the outward habit and the inner life of the Cistercians. The demesne of the nuns at Llanllŷr was compact and protected by the river and marsh, so perhaps it would have been possible for them to be involved in the farming activities, at least to some extent, in the area around the nunnery whilst retaining isolation from the outside world. The outlying lands and granges would have been managed by others, or tenanted. At the suppression of the nunnery the demesne had seven closes or enclosed areas of arable land including the old park, or Henbarc, which can still be identified by this name. Cattle on the demesne in 1536 included eight oxen, eighteen cows and fifteen cows called Hayfords, possibly Herefords. This breed of beef cattle was farmed on these pastures until twenty years or so ago.

No trace now remains above ground of the nunnery buildings at Llanllŷr, although extensive man-made ditches and watercourses provide some indication as to where the main features of the complex may have been sited. Ditches bring water from various sources to a small pond, possibly the millpond of the nunnery, to the west of the present garden. The main ditch from this continues through woodland to an area where depressions in the ground suggest that there may have been fishponds, the ditch then continuing towards the river. Various drains and other evidence suggest that the nunnery itself would have been located in the field beyond the present farmyard. The house occupied by the Lloyd family after the dissolution of the nunnery in 1536, of which a plan and the cobbled forecourt survive, was situated to the west nearer to the river, probably on the site of the infirmary. At Tintern Abbey the drain served the main complex first then continued on past the infirmary towards the river, and this may have been the case also at Llanllŷr.

What would the gardens of the nunnery have been like? The delicate white wood anemones, pale primroses and the wild daffodils which are so abundant here would have welcomed the end of winter then as they do now. The early

The lake in winter. This ornamental lake is fed from a spring in the field which was the original water source for the Nunnery millpond.

nuns followed the example of the monks in their way of life including growing their own food. If indeed the nunnery was near where the present farmyard is now situated, the vegetables, herbs and fruit could have been grown on the adjoining area, the Victorian walled garden still used today for growing vegetables and fruit. This has been long cultivated, cleared of stones and drained by stone culverts directed towards a well, which formerly provided water for the garden.

The nunnery would have had several gardens, each for a different purpose: the cloister garden, an orchard, the cellarer's garden providing food for the nuns and all those working for them, as well as guests, and an infirmary garden growing medicinal herbs. In addition the Abbess may have had a private garden and most religious houses would have had a green entrance court. Fishponds and dovecots or columbaria of stone, circular or square, would have contributed to the ambience as well as providing food for the table.

The nuns' cloister would have surrounded an area of closely cut green grass, possibly with crossing paths and with a fountain or other water source. It represented an oasis of quiet calm at the centre of the complex of buildings and was next to the church where the daily services at the canonical hours were regularly held.

On plans of some religious houses the orchard is shown by the east end of the church: examples include the nunnery at Marrick in Yorkshire as well as the monastery at Christchurch Priory, Canterbury. At Canterbury the orchard also served as the cemetery for the monks, and this may also have been the case at Marrick. The area outside the east end of the church at Strata Florida is the site of the monks' cemetery, possibly originally also an orchard. At Llanllŷr the same arrangement was probably followed. These cemetery orchards were also pleasure gardens with the fruit trees probably set out in rows with paths between, and could include roses, lilies and vines as well as meadow flowers in the grass between the trees, some of which would have been of use medicinally. At Clairvaux, at the beginning of the twelfth century, an orchard is described containing a great many different fruit trees. At Christchurch an ornamental pool was included, adding to the pleasantness of the garden and, no doubt, serving a practical purpose as well.

Most medicinal herbs would have been grown in the Infirmary garden in narrow beds which could be reached from paths on each side. At Llanllŷr, in addition to the herbarium for growing the medicinal plants needed for the infirmary, there may also have been an area, perhaps with a fountain, where the sick nuns could enjoy fresh air in pleasant surroundings and take pleasure in the scents and sounds of flowers and water.

The cellarer's garden would have been the most extensive, providing vegetables and herbs for the nunnery as well as for guests. The cellarer would also have provided honey for sweetening food and for making mead, and wax for candles, as well as the hay, rushes and other plants needed for strewing on the floor. This was essentially a utilitarian garden.

Whether the Abbess of such a small nunnery had a private garden is possibly doubtful but, if she had, it would have probably been similar to a herber or enclosed garden such as described by Albertus Magnus in his treatise *De Vegetabilibus et Plantis* of about 1260: 'the lawn is of such a size that about it in a square may be planted every sweet-smelling herb such as rue and sage and basil, and likewise all sorts of flowers, as violet, columbine, rose, iris and the like.' Such gardens were also to be found in the confined spaces within castle walls and would have been familiar to most of the gentlewomen who chose a religious life.

The courts of the princes in the twelfth century were centres in tune with the cultural awakening taking place throughout Europe. The Lord Rhys was a patron of poetry and music, holding an international competition for poets and musicians in 1176 at Cardigan, the first Eisteddfod. He also encouraged the idea of the Arthurian tradition being associated with the castle there. At the court of Marie de Champagne in France in about 1180 Cretien de Troyes wrote his Arthurian Romances in which the court of King Arthur took place at Cardigan. Lord Rhys's mother, Gwenllian, a daughter of Gruffydd ap Cynan, Prince of Gwynedd, may have been responsible for the recording of the Mabinogion, a collection of Welsh legends and myths. Elsewhere in Europe the repertoire of stories formerly included in an oral tradition of story-telling were being written down, often encouraged by the patronage of women such as Eleanor of Aquitaine, Queen of England, wife of King Henry II, and her daughter, Comtesse Marie de Champagne, the patron of Cretien de Troyes. Gwenllian may have been another cultured noblewoman associated with this trend. Some of these women also proved themselves to be formidable leaders. Eleanor of Aquitaine went on crusade to the Holy Land and proved a competent politician and ruler of her extensive lands in south-west France. Gwenllian led the defence, with her two youngest sons, of the castle of Kidwelly against the Norman Maurice de Londres. She and her sons were, however, defeated and killed.

If Llanllŷr was indeed founded by the Lord Rhys for his widowed sister Gwladus, her cultured background would have encouraged an ambience and surroundings such as she would have previously known and which would have included pleasant as well as useful gardens.

Although nothing remains of the nunnery buildings, the Cistercian ditches, drains and watercourses are still in use. One of the springs that originally supplied the millpond now provides water for our lake and Water Garden before continuing on to its original destination. Perhaps these holy women also left another less tangible legacy. A recent programme on the Welsh S4C television commented on the spiritual quality of the garden. Perhaps the spiritual aspirations of the nuns linger still. The Labyrinth in our garden reflects a spiritual quest such as theirs might have been in the allegory of the Dreamer's Journey from the fourteenth-century poem of *Piers the Plowman* by William Langland.

CHAPTER 2

Spring: Renaissance

WHEN SPRING OFFICIALLY ARRIVES towards the end of March nature begins again to clothe itself in green. The growing grass moves with the wind, the thorn puts forth its leaves and everywhere there are signs of renewed energy and excitement. With the showers of April the pace quickens and in May and June the generosity of nature is richly demonstrated in the freshness of the trees and the wildflowers in the meadows and hedgerows, as well as in the joyous songs of the birds and the frolicking of the young lambs in the fields. Each day there are exciting discoveries of renewal.

For Llanllŷr, in the sixteenth-century, there was also a change leading to rebirth and renewal. During the reign of Henry VIII and the Reformation of the church in England and Wales, the suppression of the religious houses was all-inclusive, and the nunnery at Llanllŷr was no exception. The property and possessions of the nunnery were surveyed in September 1536 and its dissolution took place soon after, on 26 February 1537.

After the dissolution the ownership of Llanllŷr passed to the Crown, which leased the property in 1537 to John Henry ap Rhydderch of Kidwelly for 21 years at an annual rental of £26 17s. 8d. He claimed possession of the land but when he tried to impose fines on the occupiers for them to remain in possession they refused to pay. At the Court of Augmentations in 1545 they claimed that they held the land by copyhold rights granted by the Abbess. The Court granted him possession, but it appears that he got neither the money nor the land. One of the occupiers was Griffith ap Henry, who had been farming Llanllŷr and continued to do so. His daughter and co-heiress, Joan or Siwan, married Hugh Llewellyn Lloyd, a third son of Castell Hywel in the south of the county of Cardiganshire (now known by its pre-conquest name of Ceredigion), who thus came into occupation of Llanllŷr.

Possibly because John Henry ap Rhydderch could not collect the money to pay the King's Auditor, a new lease was granted in 1553 to William Sakeville, esq, a server of the Queen's Board, and John Dudley, both of Dorking, Surrey. In 1554–8 Hugh Llewellyn Lloyd and John Sakevile (son of William) appeared as defendants in Chancery proceedings to answer a complaint by John Dudley, yeoman, concerning this lease.

The dissolution of the nunnery coincided with the Act of Union of Wales with England, bringing with it new prosperity to Wales and the Welsh gentry. The Act in 1536 established a uniform system of administration and law and provided for Welsh representation at Westminster. The Council of Wales and the Marches was established to deal with particularly Welsh issues. Positions in administration were open to Welshmen who increasingly took advantage of the new opportunities by sending their sons to be educated in England. Education at Oxford and Cambridge Universities led to openings in government offices, in the management of estates, in law and in the church.

At Llanllŷr Hugh Llewellyn Lloyd and his wife, Siwan or Joan, ensured that their sons took full advantage of the opportunities available. Two of their sons graduated from Oxford and went on to distinguished careers. Griffith Lloyd became Chaplain of New College in or before 1564 and the second principal of Jesus College, Oxford, in 1572. This college had been recently founded by another Welshman, Hugh Price, Ll.D, of Brecon. In 1577 Griffith was elected a Fellow of All Soul's College and was Regius Professor of Civil Law. He was MP for Cardiganshire in 1586. He presented to the College, as an endowment for the Lloyds and other Welsh scholars, various farms along the Aeron Valley, including Hendre, College, Penlan Abermeurig and Perthneuadd amongst others, some of which have only recently been sold by the College. His brother Thomas became Canon and Treasurer of St David's Cathedral in 1574 and was the father of Marmaduke Lloyd, senior Judge of the Great Sessions in Wales. Thomas's daughter Lettice married Thomas Lewes of Gernos, whose younger brother, John, bought Llysnewydd in 1610 and is the ancestor of the present family at Llanllŷr. Both Gernos and Llysnewydd are houses with estates situated to the south of Llanllŷr. In Wales it has long been the custom to identify someone by the name of the place where they live as well as by their own names.

Hugh Llewellyn Lloyd's eldest son, Morgan, remained at Llanllŷr and became a prominent Elizabethan squire. He was High Sheriff four times and was a Justice of the Peace and a Deputy Lieutenant. In 1599 he, and his kinsman Richard Price of Gogerddan, were accused by a prominent member of another county family, David Lloyd of Aber-mad, of exploiting their position to enrich themselves by obtaining a very large sum of money out of the shire armoury. Rivalry such as this between individuals jealous of each other's privileges and influence was a familiar feature of many Welsh suits heard before the Star Chamber.

Morgan Lloyd married Elizabeth, daughter and heiress of Lewis ap Henry Lloyd. Morgan died in 1604 but his widow, Elizabeth, was still living at Llanllŷr in 1613 holding one-third of her husband's estate as dower as well as two-thirds of the family estates and other property in Carmarthenshire. Their son Thomas married Lettice, grand-daughter of Richard Price of Gogerddan. They had one son who died young in 1613 and a daughter, Bridget, who became the sole heiress. She married Richard Vaughan, second Earl of Carbery, of Golden Grove (or Gelli Aur) in Carmarthenshire, who became the owner

Drawing of the Tudor house at Llanllŷr (above), identified by the heraldry of the Lloyd family to the left of the sketch. Drawing of Trawscoed (below), a house about fifteen miles from Llanllŷr. From Thomas Dineley's book *The Account of the Official Progress of His Grace Henry the First Duke of Beaufort Through Wales in 1684.*

of Llanllŷr when Bridget died childless some time before 1637, the year in which he married for the second time. After her death he exchanged Llanllŷr for other properties and a considerable sum of money with David Parry of Noyadd Trefawr, near Cardigan. With the death of Bridget the period of prosperity enjoyed by the Lloyd family at Llanllŷr came to an end, but some evidence of the house and garden from later in the century shows what they had achieved.

With the arrival of the Tudors, the Welsh gentry not only had an emotional loyalty to a monarchy of Welsh descent but also developed a growing sense of political awareness. After the Act of Union responsibility for maintaining the law at a local level greatly increased their self-confidence and sense of worth. Many families, as at Llanllŷr, had benefited from much of the wealth of the religious houses being transferred to lay people and, as aspiring, wealthy Welsh landowners wished to follow contemporary fashionable trends, inevitably attention was paid to the improvement of their homes and gardens. Old houses were either demolished and a new one built of stone with a slate roof, or a new modern wing was added to an older dwelling. These new houses had upper floors, staircases, larger glazed windows and open fireplaces. The squire's family rooms were separate from those of the servants. Some of these houses had moats for protection, or a house was built on to a courtyard surrounded by walls.

It appears that this last was the option favoured by the Lloyds at Llanllŷr. A sketch in Thomas Dineley's *Account of the Duke of Beaufort's Progress through Wales in 1684* shows a walled courtyard with a gated entrance and buildings at the further end. This sketch has been identified by the Lloyd coat of arms and the sketch of the next house in the book is labelled Trouscoad (Trawscoed), a house about fifteen miles from Llanllŷr. Both have a double, ornate iron entrance gate between smart stone gateposts; both courtyards are divided into formal rectangles edged by paths, a main path in each

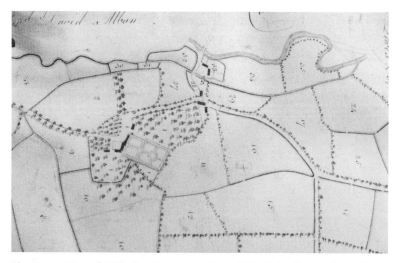

The Estate Map of 1768 showing the position of the Tudor house of the Lloyds and the garden layout.

case leading from the front gate to the main entrance door of the house. At Trawscoed this path leads up steps to a second smaller courtyard enclosed by the house on three sides.

The side wings of the two houses have a certain amount in common, although the buildings at Trawscoed are more elaborate. It is in the main central sections of the houses that there are the most significant differences. Trawcoed is a Renaissance building with a central portico with columns, pediment and gable. At Llanllŷr the central building is asymmetrical. The main entrance is shown as an extended porch with, to the left of it, a gabled, three-storey projection. This building and the wing on the right appear to reflect older buildings with some attempt to add modern features, whereas the building on the left appears more likely to have been an up-to-date new addition contributing to the comfort of the Lloyd family as well as indicating their prosperity and social pretensions. Today only the cobbled forecourt and the access drive survive.

The next piece of evidence concerning this house and its setting does not emerge until 1768, when an estate map was drawn up. David Parry died in 1642 and the house and estate subsequently changed hands several times. The estate map shows a formal garden behind the house aligned to the main building with a central axis. It is surrounded by a wall and appears to be in two parts, possibly reflecting a difference in level. The land behind the site of the house rises slightly, so each part could have been separately levelled and terraced. The smaller section near the house is bisected by a central path into two rectangular areas. This path continues into the second, larger square garden, which is divided into four equal quarters with a circular area in the centre. Paths separate and frame each section. On each side of these formal gardens wooded areas are shown together with avenues of trees leading to and from the front of the house as well as across the park to the river. The building on the left shown in Dineley's drawing of 1684 has disappeared.

The turbulent history of Llanllŷr after the death of Bridget Lloyd, before 1637, suggests that the garden is more likely to have been created during the period of greatest prosperity, when the three generations of Lloyds – Hugh, Morgan and Thomas – owned the house. Of these Morgan, at Llanllŷr 1577–1604, was the most prominent in the public life of the county, and, in addition, he had brothers in eminent positions at the University of Oxford and in the Diocese of St David's.

If Morgan and his heiress wife were responsible for the garden at Llanllŷr, they were evidently aware of contemporary trends in garden design. The quartered garden with a central feature was included in the garden at Kenilworth Castle created by Robert Dudley, Earl of Leicester. He entertained Queen Elizabeth there in 1565 and 1575. This garden has recently been reconstructed. Other late sixteenth-century gardens, such as Wollaton Hall in Nottinghamshire, begun in 1580, and Longford Castle in Wiltshire, dated 1591, also included the quartered garden.

Knot gardens in intricate designs were popular. All Soul's College, Oxford, where Griffith Lloyd was a Fellow, had complex patterns in square beds which are shown on a plan of 1585. Such patterns (also on textiles, plasterwork and other forms of decoration) were an important element in garden-making of the period. Similarly, long straight avenues of trees leading from the building as shown on the 1768 estate map are also evident in the grounds of Magdalen College according to the 1578 Agas map of Oxford.

The new fashions in gardening in England were in tune with the ideas current on the continent. In Italy elaborate gardens were created incorporating formal design and water features with adjoining woods or wildernesses. Elaborate symbolism and allegories were expressed in the design and illustrated with sculpture. The Renaissance garden in Italy was architectural, using stone and evergreen plants for the structural elements.

Some of the features found in an Italian Renaissance garden have been introduced into the present gardens at Llanllŷr. Italy is the source for the layout of the Water Garden with the open-air Stage at its western end. The Box Garden has cross-paths and a central feature. It reflects the type of patterned design found at that time in Italy and in Britain, especially below the windows of the house.

It may seem surprising that a garden reflecting contemporary ideas should be found in such a remote part of West Wales in the late sixteenth and early seventeenth centuries, although not impossible. At Aberglasney, between Llandeilo and Carmarthen and about twenty-five miles from Llanllŷr, a garden incorporating some new ideas was being created at much the same time for Anthony Rudd (1548–1615), Bishop of St David's. There a surviving elevated and arched terrace walk has been archaeologically dated to about 1600. He and Thomas Lloyd (1544–1613), Chancellor and Treasurer of St David's, would certainly have known each other.

The Box Garden by the house reflects the type of patterned design popular in the Renaissance; a similar design may have been in the garden of the Tudor house when the Lloyds lived there.

The development of the gardens at Aberglasney appears to have been continued by the Bishop's son, Rice, who is said to have been a friend of James I. The same was no doubt true of the gardens at Llanllŷr when Thomas Lloyd succeeded to the estate after the death of his father, Morgan, in 1604. Possibly the smaller of the two formal gardens at the rear of the house was there in Morgan's lifetime, and the second larger and more elaborate one was added at the beginning of the seventeenth century.

Elizabeth Lloyd, the widow of Morgan Lloyd, appears to have remained at Llanllŷr until her death in about 1615. Could she have been responsible for the development of the gardens during the early seventeenth century? She was wealthy and, as a widow, was in a position to make decisions and exercise patronage. Women were involved in garden-making at that time and books on gardening were being written and published with women in mind. Thomas Tusser's *Five Hundred Points of Good Husbandry* of 1573 included instructions to women on practical gardening, and William Lawson's *The Country Housewife's Garden* of 1618 talks of the laying out of the pleasure garden as being a job for women, including the selection of the forms of mazes and knots. There was evidently a well-established tradition that the garden was included within the sphere of influence of the lady of the house. As early as 1392–4 instructions written by an older husband, the Goodman of Paris, for his new young wife included a detailed treatise on gardening. He commented that his wife most loved to wander in her garden, weaving herself garlands of flowers, gathering fruit in season and passing on advice to the gardeners.

In Wales the gardens adjoining the state apartments at Conwy Castle are shown in a painting of about 1600 as a series of four square beds, each planted with greenery in a different pattern. Mazes and labyrinths are recorded at Gwydir Castle in Gwynedd and at Tredegar House, near Cardiff. These labyrinths would have indicated an allegorical reference, as would many of the statues or the topiary found in gardens. The allegorical labyrinth in the present garden at Llanllŷr is a reinvention of this idea.

With the Lloyds at Llanllŷr it is possible that the formal garden adjoining the house would have been planted in patterns, in knots or a labyrinth perhaps, much like the garden under the walls of Conwy Castle or at All Souls College, Oxford. These patterns would have been appreciated from above, from the windows of the house. In the second enclosed garden the quarters may have each been planted differently or, perhaps more likely, with grass and small trees planted in the corners or arranged in tubs. There would have been a feature in the centre of this garden, a fountain or statue perhaps. Some gardens had covered walkways or pergolas providing shade around the outer path, so possibly such an arrangement was also to be found at Llanllŷr, or, alternatively, fruit trees could have been grown in the shelter of enclosing walls.

On the Llanllŷr estate map woodland is shown to the north and south of the formal gardens. On the north side this would have been in the area on which it has been suggested that the original nunnery was situated, together with the nuns' orchard and cemetery. This woodland area probably represented an extended orchard. It appears on the plan as though the trees are planted in rows around a clearing. In an Italian garden of the period such a clearing would have contained a feature such as a statue and would have provided the focus for a gentle stroll, assignations or meditation. Fruit growing was widespread and much appreciated and Wales was not behind England in this respect. There are many references to orchards in Wales, one of the earliest being the description by Gerald of Wales in the late twelfth century of the orchard and fishpond at Manorbier Castle in Pembrokeshire. A survey of the orchard at Thornbury Castle in Gloucestershire in 1521 described it as being full of fruit trees, many roses and other pleasures as well as 'many goodly alleys to walk in openly'. This description has provided much of the inspiration for the development and replanting of the Old Orchard here.

On the south side of the house and formal gardens on the Llanllŷr estate map there is an area of woodland which survives today, providing shelter from the prevailing south-west winds. A clearing shown here amongst the trees is approximately where depressions are evident in the ground today, and indicate the probable site of the nunnery fishponds. It is likely that these continued to be used for this purpose by the Lloyds, as well as providing an attractive feature to the surroundings of the house. The part of the wood between the pathway adjoining the house, which is shown on the map and still exists, and the fishponds is illuminated with an extensive planting of snowdrops in the spring. Ponds were the source of fish for the household and many gardens included dovecots providing birds for the table. A late nineteenth-century diagram shows circular foundations near to the old house which may indicate a columbarium. At Old Gwernyfed in Powys, built with extensive gardens by Sir David Williams at the beginning of the seventeenth century, there were a formal quartered garden with a central feature, ponds and two circular dovecots, all of which were also evident at Llanllŷr.

The attitude of mind which delighted in the complexities of intricate patterns, labyrinths and allegories also welcomed with enthusiasm the new plants being introduced not only from the new world of the recently discovered Americas, but also those being brought to Western Europe from the Eastern Mediterranean by travellers and diplomats to the Ottoman Empire established at Constantinople. New botanic gardens to display the plants from the various different continents were established at Pisa, Padua, Montpellier, Leiden and Oxford during the sixteenth and early seventeenth centuries.

The Lloyds, with their interest in contemporary garden fashions, may well have also been collectors of some of the new plants coming into Britain at that time, but planting is too ephemeral and little evidence of their botanic interests has survived. There is, however, one possible example, as a rare double daffodil is to be found by the wood. This is similar to *Narcissus* 'Telamoneus Plenus', a rare form of a double *N. pseudonarcissus*, introduced into England in the early seventeenth century. It is also likely that the surviving snowdrops between the Tudor house and the nunnery fishponds would have been planted at that time. Snowdrops were introduced to Britain towards the end of the sixteenth century and were first recorded in Gerard's *Herbal* of 1597.

Little other evidence survives of the Lloyds' garden at Llanllŷr. Far more survived of the early gardens at Aberglasney and the restoration of these has proved to be extremely successful. They provide an example of the interest in garden-making in West Wales in this period.

CHAPTER 3

Summer: Maturity

WITH THE ARRIVAL OF summer the garden demonstrates
its richest and most colourful phase. Not only in the garden
but also in the countryside, the different greens of the trees,
hedgerows and grass bejewelled with the wildflowers that
have escaped the mower or foraging animals. Hayfields with
their rich tapestry of diverse species of flowers and grasses
enhance the landscape and set the stage for the communal
activities of the summer when, in the past, the farming
community got together to help each other with the hay-
making. The farming year is at its busiest with sheep to be
shorn and the harvest to be gathered in. The garden shows
off the roses and flower borders at their best and fruit and
vegetables are provided for the household.

At Llanllŷr it was to be another two centuries before
prosperity returned. Following the death of Bridget Lloyd and
the transfer of the estate to David Parry, debts and mortgages
as well as family quarrels led to a sad period in the history
of Llanllŷr, which was described in 1696 as being 'a decayed
house in the hands of a tenant'. After the death in 1642 of David
Parry, heavily in debt, Llanllŷr was sold to another Thomas
Lloyd, an uncle of Bridget, the heiress who married the Earl
of Carbery. Llanllŷr remained with the Lloyd family, although
mortgaged to William Sumner of Buckinghamshire, until the
death of Thomas's brother, William, in 1668, when Sumner
foreclosed, sending his son and bailiff to take possession. In
1720 the estate was sold to John Lewes, the son of a younger

The Rose Garden planted with five hundred historic roses is on the site where the long flower borders of the nineteenth-century garden were to be found. It adjoins the walled vegetable garden.

son of Llysnewydd, located on the Carmarthenshire side of the river Teifi at Henllan, which his great grandfather had purchased. He was related by marriage to the Lloyds of Llanllŷr as well as to David Parry as his grandmother, Anne, was David Parry's sister. His son John inherited Llysnewydd on the death of his cousin in 1769 and Llanllŷr was let to a tenant.

Britain in the eighteenth and nineteenth centuries was at the peak of Empire, trading across the world. Wealth from the colonies came into the country as younger sons made their fortunes and returned home to build for themselves houses and make gardens as well as founding schools and other community projects. The families who stayed in the county benefited from the increased prosperity being brought into the area and some decided to enhance their position and status by embellishing or rebuilding their houses. In West Wales other sources of increasing the family wealth might include developing mining enterprises or marrying heiresses.

John Lewes of Llysnewydd and Llanllŷr married an heiress, Rebecca, daughter of William Price of Dyffryn, near Llandybie, and through her inherited his estate. This enabled their son William to employ the services of the architect John Nash to rebuild his house at Llysnewydd in 1796. Nash was working in Carmarthen in the last decade of the eighteenth century, before moving to London and establishing himself as architect to the Prince Regent, later George IV, and becoming the most fashionable architect of the time.

The new era for Llanllŷr began in 1826 when William Lewes's third son, another John Lewes, was given the estate on his marriage to Mary Ann Vaughan Lloyd of the neighbouring estate of Brynog. This John had fought at the battle of Waterloo in 1815 in the 23rd Light Dragoons and was a noted amateur jockey, winning a number of silver cups. When John, known as 'Waterloo' Lewes, decided to build a new house at Llanllŷr it seems that he was hoping to provide a house for his wife and family in some way comparable to his childhood home at Llysnewydd. The new building was built to the east of the old Tudor house but, as the Cistercian drain continued past the new site, this may have been where the guesthouse of the nunnery originally stood. The stones from the old house were re-used with the addition of some Bath stone and some home-made bricks which had been baked on the meadows alongside the pit from which the clay was dug.

The new house is box-like with the main entrance on the north side. The east and south sides open on to lawns and on the fourth western side the service wing was hidden by shrubberies. This was similar to the arrangement at Llysnewydd and at Llanerchaeron, another Nash house about four miles down the valley from Llanllŷr. Inside the house the main rooms, as in the two Nash houses, are arranged around a top-lit inner hall with a cantilevered stair. Llanllŷr is smaller with only three reception rooms rather than four and has none of the sophisticated detailing such as curved walls or special joinery included by Nash in houses designed by him. Although Nash himself left Carmarthen in 1796, features he had introduced continued to influence the design of country houses in the area for several decades as local builders created their own versions of his designs.

Whilst at Carmarthen, Nash had working with him John Adey Repton, the son of Humphry Repton, the most fashionable contemporary landscape gardener of the time. Humphry Repton and John Nash worked together for a few years on a number of projects. In 1810 Nash, together with George Repton, another of Humphry's sons, designed picturesque cottages for Blaise Hamlet near Bristol. Designs for cottages for Nanteos near Aberystwyth have survived which have been attributed to George Repton; these have been dated to about 1813 by the watermark.

There is no firm evidence as to when the house was built. The family were all in residence at Llanllear (as the new house was then spelt to distinguish it from the earlier dwelling) for the 1841 census, with the exception of John, the eldest son, born in February 1828, who was listed as a pupil at Dr Rowley's School, Bridgnorth, Shropshire. Neither the baptism of John nor of his sister Mary, born 1836, are included in the Llanfihangel Ystrad parish register. Mary appears to have been baptised at Bristol on 31 January 1836. John Lewes evidently continued his career in the army, being referred to as a Major in 1841. Probably he was stationed at Bristol in 1836, but the fact that there was a seven-year gap between the birth of the eldest son and Mary suggests that he may have been serving abroad. Mary's birth was followed by four more siblings at yearly intervals. The third child, Thomas Lewes of Llanllear, was baptised at Llanfihangel Ystrad on 2

February 1837. The house was, therefore, probably completed before the end of 1836. Building work continued, however, on outbuildings as the date 1843 is shown on the carriage and stable block. The tithe map of 1840 shows the old house rather than the new one.

It is evident from the arrangement of the new house that the work of Nash and the houses that he designed were known to John Lewes. Similarly, the influence of Humphry Repton on various gardens and parks in the area is also apparent. Repton's parks and landscapes followed on from the earlier fashion initiated by Capability Brown who swept away the older more formal gardens to leave the house isolated in a park-like landscape. Repton re-introduced planting near the house. He kept the park but connected the house to it by means of terraces, shrubberies and enclosed gardens. Many of the gentry houses being built in West Wales at this time conformed to these ideas, including Llanllear.

The lodge at Llanllear, situated by what is now the back drive, was built in the form of a small traditional toll-house. This is in the picturesque tradition of Nash (and followed by George Repton at Nanteos) of cottage lodges designed in vernacular styles. The position of the Llanllear lodge near the bridge over the Aeron to Talsarn suggests that this may originally have been the main entrance to the new house and that the sinuous front drive may have been a later addition. The Ordnance Survey map of 1886 shows the drives and garden layout much as they remained for the next one hundred years.

A metal fence separated the lawn and drive at Llanllear from the park, but the grass of one flowed into the green sward of the other. The walled garden, possibly on the site of the nunnery garden, is near the house but hidden by a shrubbery. Gravel paths around the shrubbery lead to a long double border running the length of the outside wall of the kitchen garden.

The 1886 map shows the outline of a tennis court marked out on the lawn and a grove of trees extending across the lower edge of the lawn and into the paddock beyond. By 1905 the whole of this paddock is shown planted with fruit trees and this area remained an orchard until the 1950s.

The lack of evidence makes it difficult to ascertain which features in the garden were established by John 'Waterloo' Lewes and Mary Ann and those created by the next generation, another John Lewes (who distinguished himself at the battle for Redan in the Crimea and subsequently became known as 'Crimea' Lewes) and his wife, Mary Jane. Mary Ann died in December 1842, aged 36, only five years after moving into the new house. Perhaps the strain of having five children in five years proved too much for her, and she would, no doubt, have been much saddened by the death of her daughter Maria Cordelia, who died in October 1840 barely three years old. Mary Ann and Maria Cordelia share a memorial in the village church. Of the surviving children, the eldest, John ('Crimea') Lewes, married an heiress, Mary Jane Griffiths, from Llwyndyrys, near Cardigan, in the south of the county, in 1858 and, having bought his father out, moved into Llanllear. The second son, Thomas, went to Australia in 1856 aged twenty; the third son, Price, had a distinguished army career before settling at Tyglyn Aeron, another house further down the valley. The two daughters married into prominent local families.

Crimea Lewes and Mary Jane raised a large family at Llanllear of three sons and five daughters. Price Lewes's young daughter, Evelyn, in her book *Out with the Cambrians*, described her enjoyment as a child of a visit to her uncle at Llanllear and his cheerful wife and their handsome and high-spirited family.

As Mary Ann lived at Llanllear for only five years it is not possible to detect any particular influence that she might have had on the gardens there. It is evident, however, that, in addition to the Reptonian lawns, shrubbery and parkland by the house, the walled garden had been planted up with fruit trees, as a list of these in 1860 survives together with comments on the quality of the different fruits.

Mary Jane brought with her a copy of John Loudon's *Encyclopaedia of Gardening* (Third Edition) published in 1825. An inscription in the book reads 'John Griffiths Llwynduris 1826'. Mary Jane lived at Llanllear until her death in 1920, her husband having died in 1900. How might the gardens have developed during the sixty years that she lived there?

Certainly her large family and staff required feeding and the fruit trees, including walnut trees that survive, were planted as an orchard beyond the lawn. The children's high spirits needed outlets for their energies, so a tennis court was set out. The invention of the lawnmower in the 1830s meant that the grass could be kept short for such games and a photograph taken towards the end of the century shows the lawnmower in use, pushed by one man and pulled by another.

Some of the trees between the garden and the orchard survive but consist mainly of elderly yew (*Taxus baccata*) and silver birch (*Betula pendula*). During the nineteenth century many new plants were introduced from all over the world and there are two types of elm at Llanllear that had first appeared in Britain during that century: the Japanese and the Huntingdon elm (*Ulmus japonica* and *Ulmus* x *vergata*) which are thriving still. Two Wellingtonias (*Sequoiadendron giganteum*) were planted at the end of the long border adjoining the walled garden. These were indeed gigantic when they were felled in the 1980s for fear that they might be blown down and ruin the corner of the wall. The Wellingtonia originated in California and first came to Britain in 1853; it was named in honour of the first Duke of Wellington who had died the previous year. It became a 'must have' fashionable tree for nineteenth-century gardens.

Hay-making at Llanllŷr towards the end of the nineteenth century. The photograph was taken by Florence Mary Lewes.

Mowing the lawn at Llanllŷr around 1900 showing the tennis court marked out on the grass and various shrubs planted individually in the lawn.

Rhododendrons were also new introductions and were planted in Wales as well as Cornwall and other appropriate sites in Britain. Of the surviving elderly rhododendrons here it is not possible to be certain now as to when these were planted. It is probable that the *ponticum* in the shrubbery, in front of the house and in the woods and copses beyond the perimeter of the garden were planted in the nineteenth century before it was fully appreciated how rampant they could become. The hybrid rhododendrons along the southern and eastern sides of the lawn could have been planted then or added in the early years of the twentieth century.

After Repton the next most influential garden designer and writer was John Claudius Loudon, whose *Encyclopaedia of Gardening* Mary Jane brought with her, and which is still in the house. He emphasised the contribution of horticulture and the skill of the gardener. He encouraged the display of individual plants to the best advantage in a way calculated to show off the individual beauty of each shrub or tree. He also admired smooth, green lawns and curving, dry and firm gravel walks. It seems that the gardens at Llanllear might have met with his approval as these features were to be found there. The photograph of the lawn being mown shows large shrubs planted individually in the grass.

The visual evidence that we have of the gardens created at Llanllear in the nineteenth century is restricted to Ordnance Survey maps and one rather poor-quality photograph, together with the structure and plants that have survived. It does seem probable that the structure and design of the original Reptonian garden remained much as it was and that any additions and changes were in the planting rather than the layout.

Loudon's wife Jane wrote gardening books specifically for ladies; *The Ladies' Companion to the Flower Garden* was first published in 1840. She maintained that the creative aspects of gardening should be for the lady of the household. A woman's eye was needed for the artistic arrangement of flowers and shrubs. No doubt Mary Jane during the course of her sixty years at Llanllear would have had considerable influence on the planting of flowers in the long border adjacent to the walled garden and, very probably, fashionable island-beds of bedding plants close to the house. Such island beds still existed on the east side of the house in the 1930s.

The walled garden would have supplied fruit and vegetables for the household of family, visitors, retainers and servants. This extended for about an acre, surrounded by a cob wall erected on a stone base and protected from the weather by a tiled roof. Cob or mud walls were traditional in the valley, with most of the cottages being built in this way and thatched with reeds. The walls were painted with whitewash. These white cob walls retained enough heat from the sun to provide an ideal setting for numerous fruit trees. Along the north wall a collection of pear trees, which still survive, were selected to ripen at fortnightly intervals. Paths set at right angles divide the whole area up into rectangular sections. Apple trees were planted at corners and espaliered along the edges of the paths. Special sheds were provided for winter storage of root crops such as potatoes, as well as apples, which were laid out on stacking trays. The original greenhouses no longer survive, although the foundations indicate where they were sited along the north wall facing the sun.

In 1874 the house was enlarged to provide more accommodation for such a large family of three sons and five daughters. Hunting, shooting and fishing would certainly have been enjoyed by the male members of the family. Women as well as men would have enjoyed activities within the garden such as tennis and croquet, and the gardens would have provided a congenial setting for entertaining friends and neighbours. Archery was also a popular sport for the daughters of the house. The walk for the ladies to the summer house at the end of the long border would have been along

Watercolour of the house before it was enlarged in 1874. Painted by Mary Jane Lewes, who was born in 1862.

curving gravel paths past the shrubbery and then down the central path between the long double flower borders; a door half-way down providing access into the walled garden.

'Crimea' Lewes died in 1900 and Mary Jane in 1920. One son, Price, died in 1914, having had a successful and much-decorated career in the navy. Three of the daughters married, but the more prosperous years came to an end with the 1914–1918 war and when Mary Jane died much of the estate had to be sold for death duties and to provide for the large family. The eldest son, another John Lewes, inherited Llanllear and came to live there with his wife, Louisa Hext from Cornwall.

With the next generation the garden was maintained but it was not until some seventy years later that there was further expansion and development.

John 'Waterloo' Lewes 1796–1860

John 'Crimea' Lewes 1828–1900

Mary Jane Griffiths

John 'World War I' Lewes 1860–1932

Louisa Hext

John Hext Lewes 1903–92

Nesta Cecil Talbot

CHAPTER 4

Autumn: Here and Now

THE SPLENDOUR OF AUTUMN with its rich colours of gold, red, orange and purple amongst the different greens presents a magnificent pageant. Like an old-fashioned formal dance, a grand ball, with the ladies dressed in multicoloured silks and satins contrasting with the men in formal evening suits, the trees and late summer and autumn flowers express themselves in a shimmering kaleidoscope of colour. Autumn is the climax of the year and in the garden the vibrant hues rise in a crescendo before the garden relaxes once again into its winter rest; an appropriate metaphor, perhaps, for the garden now and in the future.

The next John Lewes and his Cornish wife, Louisa Hext, came to live at Llanllear in 1920 after the death of his mother. He was already suffering from the debilitating illness which led to his death in 1932, but Louisa continued to live on there with her daughter Gladys until 1940, when Gladys left to move into her own recently inherited house, Llanfair, on the river Teifi near Llandysul. Louisa remained at Llanllear with one servant, Jane, who had begun her service as a young dairymaid milking the house cows and progressed to becoming domestic help and an excellent cook as well as friend and support for Louisa. The garden was maintained by Tom, a skilled gardener.

Louisa was the youngest of a large family from a house called Trenarran near St Austell in the south of Cornwall. The house is still owned by the Hext family. It is situated in one of those Cornish valleys running down to the sea providing the sheltered conditions enjoyed by many important Cornish gardens. In 1906 Louisa's brother, Thomas Hext, bought Trebah, a famous garden also situated in a valley near the south coast in Cornwall. His wife, Alice, sent presents of rhododendrons and azaleas to her sister-in-law at Llanllear, but there is no record giving their names or saying exactly where they were planted.

During the Second World War part of the house was used as a hostel for the Women's Land Army and Tom, the gardener, maintained a thriving market garden providing fruit and vegetables for the local community. This contribution to the war effort and the Dig for Victory campaign took precedence over everything else and there was little time for the further development of the pleasure gardens.

Louisa was my grandmother and, as children, we very

The long flower borders in 1939, when they were maintained by Tom the gardener for my grandmother Louisa.

much enjoyed our visits to her. She was great fun and had a wonderful, if rather subversive, sense of humour. I can remember helping her to gather fruit in the old orchard beyond the garden, together with her sister-in-law, my great aunt Florence, who lived nearby in Lampeter. Louisa and Florence were both strong characters and visited each other often or talked on the telephone most days. I remember that there was problem when the price of the phone calls increased as my grandmother did not like spending money! Florence had little sense of humour, however, so Louisa usually had the last word. We used to walk with her around the garden and down the long flower borders, beautifully planted and maintained by Tom. She was very appreciative of his efforts and would stop to discuss the successes in the garden with him. He was a sought after and much respected judge of garden produce at local shows.

My father, another John Lewes, was in the Royal Navy and away for most of the war. My mother, Nesta Talbot, bought Llwyndyrys, a house about six miles from Cardigan, which was where we lived with her mother. It became a Red Cross Convalescent Hospital for the duration of the war. So far as the young members of the family were concerned this had many advantages, as we shared the catering for the staff and patients as well as the films provided for their entertainment. The garden around the house was well-planted with many interesting trees including a cork oak (*Quercus suber*) and a medlar (*Mespilus germanica*). We had ponies, a boat on the lake and enjoyed the company of other children whose families had sought the relative safety of Wales during the war. We also helped on the farm, especially during busy periods such as hay-making. There was a south-facing walled garden with a resident gardener helped by an Italian prisoner of war, Antonio from Naples, who was very kind to us children. Most of the adults were too busy with the war effort to have much time for us so we spent a lot of time with him. He helped with our own patches of garden and I can remember him encouraging me to clean my tools before putting them away. Could it have been his influence and kindness that sowed the seeds for my later love of gardening and of Italy?

In 1947 Louisa handed Llanllear over to her son, my father, and went to live with her daughter at Llanfair, taking Jane with her. My parents changed the name of the house back to its earlier spelling of Llanllŷr, and lived there for the next four and a half decades, farming and building up a pedigree herd of Jersey cows and playing an active role in county affairs but taking little interest in the garden. Tom, the gardener, stayed for a while but perhaps the lack of interest that my parents had for the garden proved to be too disheartening because, eventually, he left and moved on.

On leaving school I could not go to university as I wanted. There was no tradition in the family for university education and the alternatives offered me were to go for a year to either a domestic science or a secretarial college. I chose the latter option and then went to work in London, returning home for weekends by train. Catching the night sleeper at Paddington on a Friday night, changing at Carmarthen at about six o'clock in the morning for the Aberystwyth train and then changing trains again in Lampeter for the local train to Aberaeron, I got out at Talsarn Halt and walked down the hill arriving home in time for breakfast. After Dr Beeching's cuts these local trains disappeared and it was no longer possible to get home from London for the weekend by train. The five and a half hour journey by car after work on a Friday night was a far less attractive option. The M4 motorway to Wales had not yet been built.

In 1953 my mother answered an advertisement in the personal column of *The Times* newspaper concerning an Italian girl seeking to do an exchange visit in order to improve her English. Luisa arrived in August and spent six weeks with us in Wales and in October I went to Italy for the first time. Her family were wonderful to me, treating me like another daughter. During the following three years I probably spent more time in Italy than in Britain. It was in a sense an intellectual awakening: different ideas and priorities made me question and rationalise my own beliefs in a way that would not have occurred to me before. 'Why do you have a Queen?' I was asked. Italy had recently voted out their monarchy. I had been brought up in a service family with my father, both grandfathers, uncles and brother all in the Royal Navy or army, and serving Queen and country was a primary concern. Such questions made me think. The Queen, I felt, represented my country and its long history, whereas I appreciated that Italy was a young country. A collection of independent states, each with their own ancient history, had come together to form the country of Italy under the Kings of the House of Savoy barely a century earlier.

Luisa and her friends were students at the University in Rome. They seemed to know almost as much as I did about English literature and history, but their viewpoint was different. I was told, for example, that our Elizabethan heroes Walter Raleigh and Francis Drake were pirates! I found such differing ideas very interesting and wanted to learn and understand more about the country that I felt was becoming like a second home. I enrolled for a course in Italian Language and Culture, eventually achieving a Diploma. This included Italian history, literature and art which, combined with visits to museums and churches, gave me the grounding in art history that developed into a life-long interest.

Luisa and I, and her sister Lea, have remained close friends ever since. We visit each other regularly. Our children also have been exchanging visits and now our grandchildren are doing likewise. So that first meeting in 1953 greatly enriched the lives of three generations.

After I married we lived in London, then Suffolk, Northamptonshire and Oxfordshire, moving around as my husband Robert progressed in his career. We always returned to Wales for the children's school holidays. Initially we had a flat at Llanllŷr but latterly used a farmhouse nearby as a holiday home. Whilst in Suffolk, once our three children had started school, I found that I could get a grant to take myself to university, so I enrolled at the University of East Anglia and drove the twenty-five miles to Norwich each day to study for a degree in the History of the Visual Arts. The department there was very new and at that time offered courses in medieval, Renaissance, nineteenth-century or modern art. After the first year I chose to concentrate on the Gothic period. This has contributed to the creation of some of the references to the early history of Llanllŷr that have been included in the garden.

By the time I completed that first degree my husband was working in the Midlands and I was fortunate to get a job in the new History of Art Department being set up at the University of Warwick, where I was to remain for the next twenty years, although latterly this entailed commuting from Reading. I found the History of Art very absorbing and went on to do two further research degrees. I wonder whether I would have achieved so much if I had been able to go to university when I was eighteen, or whether the fact that I could not go then made me more determined when the opportunity arose.

In 1983 our son, Matthew, having completed a degree in Agriculture at Reading University, came to take over the farm from my father, then aged eighty, and in 1989 my husband Robert and I retired and came to look after my parents. We had been returning to Wales most weekends to oversee the modernisation and restoration of the house. We started on the newer part, that is, the 1870s extension, because the rooms were smaller, less draughty and less damp, making it easier to provide convenient and comfortable accommodation for my parents. On completing that and moving them in, we began on the older part. The restoration included redoing the roof, rebuilding the chimneys, re-rendering the outside walls, re-wiring and re-plumbing the whole house and installing central heating. In addition we put in a new staircase for my parents and made a second front door and porch to match the original. This entailed moving a lot of earth from the front of the house. The rooms on this side had originally been larders and storerooms and the earth came up as far as the windowsills, making the rooms cool but very damp. Providing for pathways along the length of the house and appropriate access to the new front door left us with two islands of earth, one large and one small. The large one contained some ancient trees, so in order to provide a suitable edging, stone walls were built around them.

In August 1987 we were able to move in, leaving the farmhouse for Matthew. We were still working and coming down for weekends but two years later we retired and were

This view of the garden in November from an upstairs window gives an idea of the spacious lawns and richness of the various autumn colours.

able to begin seriously to renovate and replant the much-neglected garden, although still dividing our time between Wales and London.

The garden as it is today represents the history of the place as well as our own interests and concerns. The development of the garden over two decades has been continuous but in order to make my description of the progress of our endeavours easier – for both writer and reader – I have divided up the various ideas into stages and related them to the seven days of the week. According to the Book of Genesis the world was created in seven days, so I have also shadowed each day of the week with the creative task achieved on that day.

Monday *Beginning*
Light out of Darkness

By the 1980s the garden really was a mess. The lawn survived, having been cut continuously by my father with a sit-on mower which managed to destroy any plants intruding into its path. A gift of a magnolia planted by a kind friend one winter lasted only until mowing started again in the spring. Perhaps my father just did not see it or perhaps it was too difficult to manoeuvre the mower around it at speed.

The three ancient rhododendrons planted individually on the east side of the lawn were being stifled by full-grown wild elder. The shrubbery was a thicket of *ponticum* rhododendrons and brambles. The long borders were a sad neglected wilderness. The fruit trees in the orchard, except for three magnificent walnut trees, had been grubbed out to provide a passageway for my father's precious Jersey cows, who had left an inevitable legacy of docks behind them. The area between the garden and the orchard was also an unruly tangle of seedling sycamore, holly, elder and brambles.

How and where to start was a problem we postponed worrying about as the house needed attention first. In

December 1985 Matthew fired the starting gun for the garden by taking a bulldozer into the shrubbery, clearing everything away except for one ancient Japanese flowering cherry with candy-pink blossom (*Prunus* 'Kanzan'). We arrived down for the weekend to be greeted with: 'There you are – now you can start planting.' We had been that year to Exbury, on the south coast of England, for a most enjoyable lunch with Edmund de Rothschild, who had shown us around the gardens there. We sought the advice and help of the garden director, drawing up plans and ordering plants. With a gang of helpers and friends the planting was accomplished in the following spring. The area was mulched and we celebrated what we hoped was a successful couple of weekends' work. Alas, we did not realise that the situation of the garden at the bottom of the valley meant that it is in a serious frost pocket, and late spring frosts the following year did wreak havoc with some of the early-flowering rhododendrons and magnolias as well as the hydrangeas. We had to adapt our thinking and find alternatives, but it taught us a valuable lesson. Plants from the milder climate to the south did not necessarily appreciate our cooler, wetter conditions, whereas plants from the colder, drier areas of East Anglia or the Midlands enjoyed the more temperate and moister environment.

Although I had gardened in East Anglia, the Midlands and in the Thames Valley, I had not expected such problems. But problems provide challenges and I found that I could grow early flowering shrubs to the north of the house, where they were more sheltered. This is also where I can see and enjoy them whenever I leave the house by the front door, as this was very wisely situated on the north side so that visitors coming to call in their carriages were protected from the prevailing south-west wind.

How could I protect the planting on the south side from the devastating effects of the late spring frosts? Shelter belts of some sort seemed to be required, so we planted a shrub border in 1989 on the east side of the lawn beyond the line of the original park fence, taking into the garden an additional strip of land from the adjoining field. Also a planting of evergreen shrubs and a weeping birch (*Betula pendula* 'Youngii') were established at the corner of the house to protect the plants by the south wall. It took me some time – I think it was about fourteen hours altogether – to plan out the planting for the north and east shrub borders. I chose plants that I had used before in our earlier gardens, particularly the one in Northamptonshire, and aimed to create a tapestry effect of different coloured leaves and textures. Flowers are a bonus as their contribution is more fleeting, and, consequently, all the more appreciated. Coloured stems for winter interest are included as well as a good proportion of evergreens. All the trees and shrubs for the north and east borders were ordered from a nursery in Suffolk and have proved to be very successful.

The Terrace and East Shrub Border framing the lawn near the house.

We also planted the two islands on the north side at the same time. The large island had two ancient conifers and a weeping willow. We added camellias and small Japanese maples, and an extensive collection of winter cyclamen, hellebores and bulbs. This area is at its best in the winter months.

On the south side of the house we terraced the area with a curving wall, creating a paved space near the house and a semi-circular lawn enclosed by planting. Steps leading down from the terrace to the main lawn are flanked by balls of box (*Buxus sempervirens*). To the west, beyond the terrace, a circular box garden was included to provide an interest for my parents, whose sitting-room windows looked down on it from the first floor. In the design of this I wanted to reflect some element of the Lloyds' garden, so I divided the circle with cross-paths and included a central feature. Initially this was an ancient sundial, later moved to the rose garden and replaced with a pot containing a spikey cordyline (*Cordyline australis*). How was I going to fill the spaces formed by the four quarters? Annual bedding plants seemed too obvious a solution so I looked again for some historical idea from the Italian Renaissance gardens that I knew. Statuary or topiary was often used then to symbolise references to the family or owners in some way, perhaps by initials or heraldic arms, so I added box plants within the segments to form letters indicating a name. For height I added box lollipops in each of the outer corners. This proved to be a happy solution until the dwarf box I was using (*Buxus sempervirens* 'Suffruticosa') decided it did not like our damp climate and started turning brown in patches. It has now been replaced by a form of Japanese holly (*Ilex crenata* 'Convexa').

Planting the border on the east side of the lawn had provided the impetus for removing the elder and rhododendrons long established there. It would have been impossible to remove the elder without destroying the rhododendrons as well, but we had been reluctant to remove such long-established plants. The rhododendrons along the south side of the lawn had survived the ravages of time in rather better shape, although the wilderness around them needed sorting out. Seedling hollies and birch were removed together with brambles and nettles, and a wall was built to retain and separate the rhododendrons from the area beyond.

Once the earlier planting in the shrubbery had begun to get established, after about three years, we planted ground-cover plants including various hardy geraniums, alchemilla, smaller periwinkles, symphytum or comfrey, epimediums, pulmonarias and wood anemones. There were already sheets of the native bluebell in May as well as some narcissus and snowdrops for earlier in the season. We have added more snowdrops each year, transferring clumps of the Lloyd family's plantings in the wood.

I like that sense of continuity. They increase and spread themselves happily in both places. We have also added winter flowering cyclamen and martagon lilies, the only lilies I have succeeded in growing in our damp, acid soil. The shrubbery is an area of about half an acre that is full of interest all the year round. I have included narrow paths winding through it so that it can be enjoyed whatever the season.

By Easter 1990 the essential areas around the house and lawn had been renovated and planted establishing the framework for this part of the garden. It was time to move on to new challenges.

Tuesday *Vistas*
Heaven and Earth

Beyond the rhododendrons on the south side of the lawn, in a low swampy area, there was a ditch that originally carried the water from a spring in the field on the east side of the garden to the nuns' millpond beyond the end of the long borders. The length of the ditch was a wilderness of nettles, brambles and other self-sown thugs. Robert wanted a lake and I wanted an Italian water garden so we needed to find a way of transforming this unpromising space in a way that would satisfy us both.

A lake or large fishpond, about the size of an Olympic swimming pool, was dug out by a large digger in the summer of 1989. Nine feet of peat were removed before reaching the clay subsoil. The eastern end of the ditch was cleaned out for about ten yards from where the water entered the garden, carried along underground pipes from the spring in the field, to where it entered the lake. This allowed for an area of bog garden bisected by a path leading to a wooden bridge over the ditch. Primulas raised from seed were planted in this area, together with other appropriate bog plants such as gunnera, petasites, ferns and irises. The primulas, originally *japonica* 'Miller's Crimson' and 'Postford White' and *bulleyana* have intermingled and now present in early summer wonderful expanses of various pastel shades.

At the other end of the lake a dam was built and faced with stone. The view from the dam, known as the Causeway, looking east towards the bridge and newly planted bog garden, provided the first vista or focal point in the areas of the garden which lay beyond the immediate surroundings of the house.

The next challenge was to be the creation of the Italian water garden. In the early 1980s I was fortunate in having a grant from the British School in Rome to study and photograph the Renaissance gardens there for the Photograph Archive in the History of Art Department at the University of Warwick. I very much enjoyed and admired the structure of these gardens, although attempting to transpose such ideas to a country garden in wild Wales might not prove wholly appropriate. At first the chaotic, sunken muddle of a ditch choked with weeds, nettles and brambles offered little hope that anything remotely reminiscent of the wonderfully architectural gardens that I had seen in Italy could be re-created here. We had to clear the area before we could work out any plans for the future, so the digger was brought in and the undergrowth removed. We found a traditional stone-faced bank on the side by the long border. On the other side the ground sloped gently up towards some ancient yew trees.

Helping us with the building work was a skilled and creative craftsman, Peter, from Devon. He suggested that serpentine walls around this sunken area would provide a stronger solution on the rather boggy ground, adding that he had always wanted to build one but had not had the opportunity before. It was a brilliant idea. Seven circles of thirty feet provided the basic plan. Along the length of this area Peter created a narrow one-foot-wide water channel or rill using ready-mixed concrete. At the eastern end the water from the lake flows through a lion's mouth into three descending stone-built basins and thence into the rill. At the western end the wall formed the edge of a green Stage such as those found in some Italian gardens. At the back of the Stage we planted four 'Skyrocket' junipers to remind us of Italian cypresses that, unfortunately, are not hardy enough to grow in this climate. Across the diameter of the central circle Peter made a cobbled path descending from circular steps each side and crossing the rill by a low hump-backed bridge. The adjoining circles each contain a twelve-foot-diameter hexagonal pool with a central fountain.

A yew hedge was then planted all along the top of the wall, except for the western green stage end, with an extra plant on each of the convex curves so that the hedge on the water garden side could be shaped to follow the shape of the wall. *Cotoneaster salicifolius* 'Gnom' and variegated ivies were planted on the wall and, as they have grown downwards, now hide the grey covering of concrete on the walls. The yew hedge provides a barrier hiding the water garden from

The Rill and Water Garden are based on ideas from Italian gardens.

immediate view. This creates a surprise for a visitor to the garden and provides a tranquil green space to contrast with the more colourful areas. In summer pots of red begonias are arranged along the edges of the rill and in the old cast-iron hoppers or tops of the down-pipes from the house, which had been replaced during the restoration, placed now in the concave curves of the serpentine wall. Colours in this area are restricted to green and red.

At the eastern end near the lion's head there is a small gravelled area with a seat, providing a peaceful place to sit, admire the vista and listen to the trickling flow of water. Close by there is a sloping gap in the wall and hedge for the lawnmower or wheelbarrow to enter and leave.

This sunken water garden is parallel to the area that previously contained the long flower borders of my grandmother's day and the renovation of these was to be our next project. At the western end there was a dilapidated wooden summerhouse long past repairing; we decided to replace it with a more permanent edifice that could double as an orangery in winter and provide shelter for our more tender plants.

Here Peter devised an attractive and very useful building with glazed doors facing both down the borders and on to the stage, and double-glazed windows on the west side towards the nuns' millpond and the wood. Cavity walls and insulation in the roof space provide enough protection from the cold winter weather for no further heating to be needed. Frost-tender lemon and orange trees, oleanders and olives survive here in pots during the winter. In summer they go outside on to the stage, standing by the south side of this pavilion or summerhouse. This building can then come into its own for summer entertaining or just as a peaceful retreat.

The summerhouse closes the vista along the long borders. These were planted in the autumn of 1990 with a collection of five hundred historic roses under planted with complementary perennials. The planting scheme was devised for us by Hazel le Rougetel, the historic rose expert, whom we approached for help after attending one of her lectures at the Chelsea Physic Garden. The colours flow from white at each end through apricot, pale pink, dark pink to crimson at the centre. The smell of roses during their peak season in summer is truly intoxicating, more intense perhaps because of the enclosed space with the wall on one side and the yew hedge on the other.

One last feature that Peter created for us was a circular arbour at the back of the old orchard. Again we wanted a focal point for the views to and from, firstly, the house, secondly, the door into the walled garden framed by the gaps in the yew hedge for the steps into and out of the water garden, and, thirdly, across towards the stage. Later we framed these views with avenues of flowering trees (*Malus* x *robusta* 'Red Sentinel' and *Prunus* 'Taihaku'). It was a matter of discussion as to the form this focal point should take. Robert had seen a ruined tower in a garden at the Chelsea Flower Show but Peter's professional pride was such that he could not bring himself to build a ruin. So we had a circular laburnum arbour instead, with late-flowering clematis. The local blacksmith made the metal frame and Peter cobbled the floor with a design radiating from the centre. Two seats encourage rest and contemplation.

Peter felt that this area needed a name and had some white stones that he could incorporate into the cobbled floor. I had just come back from Italy where I had visited Assisi, so this is the name written across the entrance. Later a small statue of St Francis was placed at the back of the arbour together with a few small stone animals given to us as gifts. Small children enjoy rearranging these!

The structural work in the garden had now been completed and our next challenges were to be with plants and planting, developing various spaces with new projects.

Wednesday *Allegory*
Plants and Planting

From 1989, for a few years, we greatly benefited from the help of John, a gifted gardener. With his help the north and east shrub borders were planted as well as the rose garden and the bog garden. He also helped plant trees and shrubs along the new drive. The old drive had exited on to the road on a corner which had become very hazardous with the increasing volume of traffic so, in 1990, the drive was extended along the inside of the hedge to provide a safer way in and out by exiting on a straighter section of the road. John raised many plants from seed and the garden thrived under his care. It was very much our loss when he decided that his future lay with caring for people rather than for plants and took up nursing. The intensive care unit in our local hospital gained considerably from his decision.

The major planting and structural schemes had been completed by the time Peter and John moved on, but there were still areas of the garden where we could develop further features. Over the years we have created additional areas of interest with the part-time help of Lucy and Derek. Lucy looks after the plants with much care and commitment whilst Derek, another talented craftsman, does whatever is needed in the way of woodwork as well as cutting hedges or pruning trees and shrubs. Both are invaluable and have been helping us now for about fifteen years. There are always improvements to be considered and I find it a great help to be able to talk through ideas with Lucy, who knows the garden as well as I do.

The next major development that we undertook with their help was the creation of a labyrinth. Matthew was the first to suggest that we included some form of maze in the garden but I did not want a maze of the sort to be found at Hampton Court or Glendurgan in Cornwall, where having difficulty in finding one's way out was a feature of the design. I felt that I wanted a theme or story with a beginning and an end and interesting features along the way. Historically labyrinths have been associated with allegories, so we decided that our labyrinth would be loosely based on the spiritual journey of the Dreamer in *Piers the Plowman*, the fourteenth-century poem by William Langland that I happened to be reading at the time that we were looking for ideas. The theme of this poem has been compared to Dante's *Divine Comedy* and Milton's *Paradise Lost* as well as *Pilgrim's Progress* by John Bunyan. Such a theme seemed appropriate here and would connect with the time when the nuns devoted their lives to just such a quest, and also to the Renaissance garden of the Lloyds when allegories were an essential component in the culture of the time.

There was a rather unprepossessing area in the old orchard, adjoining the yew hedge, where the stumps of old yew trees and silver birches, underground springs and persistent brambles and weeds made maintenance difficult. About a quarter of an acre in extent and hidden from the main part of the garden, this seemed to be an ideal site to be developed into our Labyrinth. Until the spring of 1998 we were still spending a lot of time in London and it was there, in between hours spent in libraries researching the artistic initiatives of medieval women that I worked out the design and details of our new project. That autumn we marked out a wedge-shaped area, having cleared it first, and erected a windbreak net screen around it so that the following spring the area was ready for planting.

The plan of the Labyrinth consists of a path connecting a number of small garden rooms, some of which lead no further. Each area has a different planting scheme as well

The design of the Labyrinth was inspired by the fourteenth-century allegorical story of *Piers the Plowman* by William Langland. The Golden Garden, seen here, is at the end of the Dreamer's Journey.

as clues, references and emblems illustrating the allegorical story of the Dreamer's journey.

The story is complex and detailed. It begins with the poet dreaming of the plain of this world set between the Tower of Truth and the Dungeon of Falsehood. He dreams of Reason, who is preaching repentance to the crowd of people on the plain and especially to each of the Seven Deadly Sins: Envy, Avarice, Lust, Greed, Sloth, Wrath and Pride. The Dreamer goes on to seek Do Well, Do Better and Do Best and in his search encounters Thought, Intelligence, Learning, Fortune, Imagination and Patience amongst many other characters. Eventually he meets Faith, Hope and Charity. He dreams of Christ's Passion as described in the Gospels and finds Peace, one of the four daughters of God.

Each room leads through to another one but there are choices to be made along the way and the wrong choice will lead into a room with no other exit. These are the rooms occupied by the Sins and in each of these there is a bench on which to sit and rest or contemplate. The last room through which one walks towards the exit is the largest and contains a metal gazebo and seats.

The outer boundary of the Labyrinth is planted with *Ligustrum ovalifolium* and the inner hedges are *Escallonia* 'Donard Seedling'. Trees planted include *Cercis canadensis* 'Forest Pansy', *Elaeagnus* 'Quicksilver', *Prunus serrula*, *Halesia monticola*, *Malus hupehensis* 'John Downie', *Sambucus porphyrophylla* 'Black Lace', *Magnolia wilsonii*, *Stewartia pseudocamellia* and *Cornus controversa* 'Variegata'. For the underplanting the emphasis is on foliage, but some flowers indicate the colour spectrum, so by following the colours of the rainbow one finds the right path. At the entrance to the Labyrinth are the orange roses 'Soleil d'Or' and 'Warm Welcome'. The colour trail continues with scarlet, crimson, purple, blue, acid green and finishes with the final golden garden containing the gazebo planted with passion flowers,

Passiflora caerulea. The dead-end rooms dedicated to the sins have no flowers but the foliage is dark green in one, blue-green in another and bronze in the third.

Allegories and symbolism played a role in our culture over many centuries but are out of fashion in this materialistic age and this area of the garden evokes very differing reactions. Some people find the concept interesting, others have difficulty with the sentiment inherent in allegory, but amongst children this is almost invariably the favourite part of the whole garden. Perhaps it is the element of secrecy that they find appealing or the intimate scale compared with the wider spaces outside and perhaps they enjoy the many little figures of people and animals representing the various sins and personifications.

The plants in the Labyrinth have been carefully selected to contribute to the story but the selection of plants in such fertile, moisture retentive soil presents challenges as well as triumphs. Some plants thrive and quickly establish themselves, growing so rapidly that regular pruning is essential. Plants from south-east Asia mostly do well, but plants from dryer, warmer regions such as lavender or ceanothus do not like our damp conditions and only survive for a comparatively short time.

Beyond the exit from the Labyrinth is a gravel garden that was one of the features developed later in connection with particular family events and anniversaries.

Thursday *Markers*
Seasons and Days

In 2002 the Queen's Golden Jubilee was celebrated, so the Jubilee Walk seemed to be an appropriate name for a new path and planting created that year along the north side of the lake. We had been gradually developing this area. Initially the lawn had sloped down to the water's edge, but when our grandchildren started riding their bicycles on the lawn we were concerned that one of them might not be able to stop in time and would end up in the water. Derek erected a wooden post and rail fence with gates at appropriate places along its length. This gave me an excuse to plant another shrub border along the fence on the lawn side. There is a gap, with a gate, between the rhododendrons and the newer border through which one can glimpse the water beyond, and a much broader double gateway leading on to the Causeway.

The area of grass between the fence and the water was difficult and awkward to mow so we made a path with a raised bed on the fence side and a narrow bed on the other side with a lower level again at the water's edge. The levels are separated and retained with wooden sleepers. On the fence side we planted *Nepeta* 'Six Hills Giant' and the long-flowering *Hemerocallis* 'Stella de Oro'. The other side of the path is planted principally with *Hemerocallis lilioasphodelus* and *Crocosmia* 'Jackanapes' together with varieties of rodgersias, sanguisorbias and astrantias. The lowest level by the lake contains collections of various irises and marginal plants such as *Pontederia cordata*, *Caltha palustris*, *Lysichiton americanus* and *Lysichiton camtschatcensis*. This Jubilee Walk faces south, getting the full benefit of the sun and the planting has proved very successful.

Also in 2002 we celebrated one of those landmark birthdays. To mark the occasion Robert and I decided to commission something special for the garden. Using a piece of our own oak, a talented local wood carver created what we wanted. It was to be positioned opposite the exit from the Labyrinth and we asked that the Welsh word 'Tangnefydd' meaning peace should be incorporated into it. This was carved around the base of the column of oak forming a kind of root system from which the rest of the decoration could be supported. A quotation from St Paul – 'The Fruits of the Spirit are Love, Joy, Peace' – curves up around the column surrounded by carvings of flowers and vines.

The shadow of the carved oak column in the gravel garden at midday marks the months of the year, each month being indicated by a circular mosaic sign of the Zodiac.

Some time after this column had been installed we realised that the sun fell on it only at midday. For a year, when the sun obliged, we measured the length of the shadow each month. Having seen a meridian marked by the sun each month at the Naples National Museum, this gave us the idea of marking the months of the year by doing something similar here. The full extent of the fall of the shadow of the column at noon was marked out, edged with wood and filled with white pebbles. I made circular mosaics of the signs of the Zodiac using black and white stones and these were placed amongst the white pebbles as our monthly measurements indicated. The fall of the shadow measures only one yard in June but ten yards in December.

Having set out the meridian, the area around it needed to be developed. There was an elderly yew nearby, half of which had died, so we had a seat made in that part, and kept the live part of the tree as a backrest. We then gravelled the area around the yew with the meridian marking the boundary, and formed a complementary gravelled area on the other side adjoining the hedge boundary of the Labyrinth, leaving a grass path to the steps down to the water garden. There were already some shrubs planted near the yew hedge and further planting was included in the gravel. The area is shaded for most of the day and the ground is moisture-retentive, but selections of hostas, hardy geraniums and other carefully selected plants have thrived in these conditions.

We also chose to mark an important wedding anniversary by placing a seat on the Causeway against the yew hedge where we could sit and look across the lake towards the bridge at the other end. The seat was placed within a wooden pergola made by Derek over which we are growing the fragrant David Austin rose The Generous Gardener. Beds on either side have been planted with grasses and late summer perennials as well as tulips and alliums to provide interest earlier in the year.

Such markers contribute to a personal record of our own stewardship of the garden and help to record the passing years, seasons and days.

Friday *Success*
Birds and Beasts

2004 was a year of success. Our efforts were recognised within Wales when we were short-listed for the Welsh television S4C *Clwb Garddio* competition for the best gardens in Wales. S4C is the Welsh-language channel in place of the Channel 4 that is available in England, and *Clwb Garddio* translates as Garden Club. It was a very interesting experience with the three judges visiting each of the short-listed gardens in turn. We found their comments and opinions very helpful in focusing our minds on the good points of the garden and on where there were areas that we should work on to improve.

We met together at Caernarfon at the end of the summer to hear the results. Four competitors had been short-listed for each of the two categories, for a large or a small garden. We were delighted, and surprised, to win the prize for the best large garden. All the competitors were given Portmeirion china but the winner in each group also received a prize of £1000. We enjoyed spending time during the following winter in puzzling over the problem of how we were going to spend this prize and deciding where in the garden would benefit from this unexpected gift. We wanted to have one definite objective that we could identify with this success, rather than several different ideas spread around the garden. We decided to develop the area by the summerhouse that we called the Stage.

The green Stage at the end of the water garden at this point

The Stage has paving in a design found in medieval Roman churches and in Westminster Abbey, two surprise water geysers, and statues of the Four Seasons. This arrangement was created after we won the prize for 'the best large garden in Wales' in 2004 in a competition organised by S4C Welsh television.

in time was simply lawn and four 'Skyrocket' junipers. It was difficult to mow and required the small lawnmower used for the water garden rather than the large one used for the rest of the extensive lawns. Robert was delighted and relieved when I suggested that we paved this area, doing away with any future need to bring the small lawnmower all the way to this awkward spot.

We returned the following May from a visit to the Chelsea Flower Show with the names of a couple of suppliers of paving stones whose products we had admired in the show gardens. One of them had a designated agent near here whom we contacted and who agreed to do what we wanted. I had settled on a design that I had come across during the course of some historical research many decades earlier into the work of the Roman craftsmen brought to England in the thirteenth century to work on King Henry III's new Abbey at Westminster. The design, consisting of one large circle with four small interlocking circles, is found in many medieval churches around Rome, and in the presbytery pavement in Westminster Abbey. At Westminster an inscription in Latin is included telling us that Abbot Ware brought the stones for the floor from Rome and that it was made by the Roman marble-worker Odericus in 1268. The inscription also explains the meaning of the design. The large circle represents the macrocosm or universe and the smaller circles the microcosm or mankind. In medieval times the interpretation would indicate the meeting place between heaven and earth and, personally, I feel that this interpretation is entirely appropriate to the way that I feel about my own garden. In modern day terms it could be interpreted as the relationship of man to his environment.

The circles consisting of pre-cut sections of stone of slightly varying hues were put in place and linked by encircling bands of slate. The surrounding area was covered with golden-coloured gravel. A flowerbed was created around the

'Skyrocket' junipers and edged with stone. On another visit to the Chelsea Flower Show Robert found a cylindrical stainless steel fountain about four feet high that he bought for our new enterprise. This was erected in the centre of the flowerbed, with flanking stainless steel balls. We placed statues of the Four Seasons between the junipers. We planted *Heuchera* 'Red Spangles' along the front with *Ophiopogon planiscapus* 'Nigrescens' around the stainless steel in the centre. Behind these plants *Tulipa* 'Red Riding Hood', *Hemerocallis* 'Stafford', *Crocosmia* 'Lucifer' and *Schizostylis coccinea* provide a succession of red flowers from spring to autumn. The planted area was then covered with a slate mulch complementing the slate used for the encircling bands on the paving.

The statues of the Four Seasons provided another echo of our interest in Italian gardens. Robert would also have liked to include water jokes of the sort we had seen in Italy – another Renaissance concept – but after a lot of discussion we felt that perhaps Wales did not have the right climate. Enough rain comes from the skies without adding the risk of being soaked by an unexpected spray, but a surprise that startled with the sudden noise of a surge of water would be more acceptable. Accordingly geyser fountains were installed on each side and connected to a sensor in the centre that detects movement. As the unsuspecting visitor moves across the stage the two jets of water erupt, causing considerable surprise.

Mediterranean plants in pots stand by the summerhouse from May until October, when they are moved inside for the winter. By these there is a seat where one can sit and enjoy the vista up the water garden, listening to the sound of the water trickling down the cylindrical fountain and to the sounds of the birds singing in the woods beyond.

The woods also provide homes for animals that are definitely not so welcome in the garden. Badgers dig holes in the grass. Grey squirrels strip trees of their bark, killing off the tops. They act without warning – usually on just one night in June – and are particularly destructive of acers of all kinds. They seem to prefer those that have been established for ten years or so; not the very young or the very old, but the adolescent trees. Perhaps the most tiresome of all are the rabbits. Twenty years ago when we started to garden the rabbit population had not recovered from the ravages of myxomatosis, but they have been creeping back and are now a real nuisance. We planted up the triangular areas between the avenues of flowering trees with waves of the purple moor grass (*Molinia caerulea*) but each spring we have to battle with the rabbits as they chew on the young growth. We set children's plastic windmills amongst the grasses in the hope that the noise they make as they whirl around with the wind would deter the rabbits. Maybe it does a bit, but not on quiet nights when there is no wind. Moles are also an increasing menace, travelling ever further under the lawns, but at least I know that their presence suggests a healthy population of worms which in turn indicate a soil in good heart.

There are many birds, animals and insects that are very welcome in the garden. We enjoy listening to the songs of the birds and watching the antics of the ducks and moorhens on the lake. When I work in the garden a robin usually keeps me company and kites fly above wheeling gracefully across the sky watching what I am doing. They nest in the wood beyond the garden. Herons also nest there and like to wait statue-like on the jetty by the lake hoping for fish to venture within reach. They are very regular in their habits and eight o'clock in the morning and four o'clock in the afternoon seem to be their favourite times of the day. The frogs and hedgehogs are very much to be encouraged, particularly on account of their partiality for eating slugs. Gardens need bees and ladybirds. All are part of the integral fabric of the garden along with the plants and all represent the continuity of the natural world.

Saturday *Continuity*
People

Nature and the natural world have evolved continuously over millions of years and will continue to do so unless some incredible catastrophe occurs. There is also a very strong sense of the continuity of history here. The history of the place has been described in the earlier chapters, but the origins and continual presence of my own family in this part of west Wales also go back at least eight centuries. A L Rowse, the historian, describing his own roots in Cornwall said that his family had been there 'since Adam was a child'. I can understand his comment. With such a strong sense of continuity in this place and in this part of Wales, we sought an opportunity to mark and emphasise our appreciation with an appropriate symbol in the garden.

In the nineteenth century two Huntingdon elms (*Ulmus x vergata*) were planted in the corner of the old orchard near the eastern boundary but during a winter gale one of these blew down. After the fallen tree was cleared away the stump was left collecting brambles and nettles in its embrace. When Matthew was removing the topsoil from the Stage prior to it being paved, he asked whether I would like him to put the earth anywhere. I suggested putting it on top of the stump to create a Mound.

The Mound is not large; about five feet high and about twelve feet in diameter. There is a circular gravelled area about three feet across on the top accessed by narrow steps on the far side. A gravelled path encircles the base. We planted the sides with *Persicaria affinis* to provide a weed-suppressing groundcover. The shiny neat green leaves of this plant reflect the light and the flowers with their pink deepening to red candles put on a show from midsummer to autumn. In autumn the leaves turn a rich brown, lasting throughout the winter like those of a beech hedge.

The Mound was created over a tree stump using the topsoil from the Stage. The circular sculpture on the top is intended to symbolise the continuity of history, time and natural world. The plant with the pink flowers is *Persicaria affinis*.

The Mound provided the pedestal for the sculpture that we wanted. We were looking for a design that would symbolise the continuity of history, time and the natural world, preferably in a circular form. We eventually found a suitable sculpture, entitled 'Flame', made of pale, polished granite. The circular form provides a view through to the hills beyond and fulfils our desired effect perfectly. To draw the eye towards it we planted *Leucothoe fontanesiana* 'Scarletta', three on each side to frame the approach to the mound with their humps of evergreen leaves, copper red in winter.

This sculpted Flame, symbolising continuity, also stands as a memorial for all those who have lived and gardened here and enjoyed this wonderful and precious place. The inscribed stone reminds us of the early hermits and we are ever conscious of the benign but unseen presence of the nuns whose spirits live on. The snowdrops planted by the Lloyds provide a continual reminder of their time here. Our own pleasure in the house and garden reminds us of the contribution of my own ancestors who built it and were responsible for the initial layout of the garden as well as the succeeding generations that nurtured and enjoyed it in its beautiful setting.

Sunday *The Future*
Rest

No garden is ever finished. Restricting over-exuberant plants and replanting unsuccessful or congested areas are jobs that need continual attention. The emphasis here is on low maintenance and we garden organically as far as possible. Mulching with composted bark helps to suppress weeds and, where appropriate, ground-cover plants are extensively used.

Long before we began gardening here, my grandmother and her daughter Gladys planted many large-flowered daffodils along the line of the fence separating the lawn from the field. John the gardener dug all these up and replanted them in the grass by the drive, where they look splendid in spring amongst the collection of birch trees that we planted there. Such contributions to the garden by family members, where they can be identified, provide precious connections between the past and the present. A magnificent oak tree just beyond the end of the lawn was planted by my father as a child about a hundred years ago. My grandson Joshua, aged ten, collects the seedlings from beneath it to add to his collection of seedling chestnut and beech trees which he and his brother George, aged eleven, sell when the garden is open for charity once a year in June. Perhaps they will be entrepreneurs one day but, whatever the future holds, the continuity from one generation to another is reassuring.

No garden can stand still frozen in a moment of time. It is a continual process of planting, correction and renewal. Plants need replacing, gaps need filling and over-exuberance needs disciplining. Within the boundary of the garden a great many smaller bulbs have been planted to complement our collections of hellebores and cyclamen, and more are added each year. Some plants thrive in our damp climate and fertile soil, others hate it. Sun-loving plants such as lavenders or ceanothus last a few years and then have to be replaced, or alternatives found. For those of us who enjoy gardening, it is a constant, exciting and rewarding challenge.

For the moment we have succeeded in establishing the various goals that we set out to achieve, but can we yet say that there are no more projects for us to aim for? For the time being we can rest and enjoy the garden that we have created.

From the seat between late summer flower borders one can enjoy the view over the Causeway across the lake. The Celtic inscribed Stone is just visible in an alcove in the wall on the right of this picture, partially framed by the hanging berries of *Sorbus commixta*.

Perhaps next year we might terrace the slope on the far side of the lake, and there is a corner beyond the walled garden that might be an appropriate site for the creation of a garden of the senses. That area is occupied by a family of pigs at present so there is no urgency, but perhaps one day it might be possible.

After my parents died in the early 1990s Matthew moved into their part of the house with his wife and young family. He also took over the walled garden, where he grows fruit and vegetables organically for sale, as well as for his family. This is an enterprise that may well develop further when time permits.

What of the future? Will this garden return to sleeping mode waiting for the next enthusiastic gardener to take it in hand once again? Or will the next generation of the family continue to maintain, expand and enjoy it as we have? Matthew has contributed many very helpful ideas for the development of the garden, but as a working farmer he has little time for a hands-on approach to pleasure gardening. Our other son, Patrick, has set up a business bottling water of exceptional quality from an underground source that may well have been supplying the occupants of this place for many centuries. He markets and exports the water, taking the name 'Llanllŷr SOURCE' around the world. Perhaps one day in the future it may prove possible for some such enterprise to enable the maintenance of the garden to continue.

We are each of us links in a chain, and the next guardians of this precious place must adapt to the times in which they live and to the circumstances in which they find themselves. From time to time during the course of the preceding centuries the gardens here have been nurtured and cared for and we can but hope that such times will come again in the future.

GENEALOGIES

Lloyds of Llanllŷr circa 1500-1700

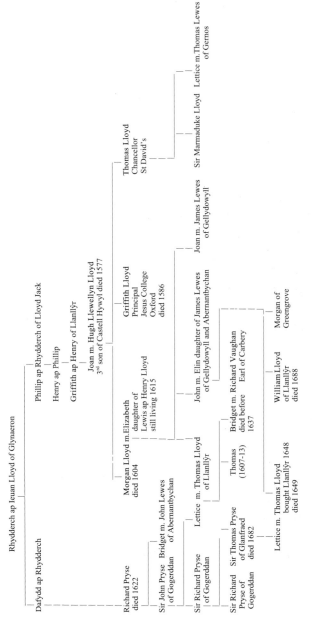

Rhydderch ap Ieuan Lloyd of Glynaeron

Dafydd ap Rhydderch

Phillip ap Rhydderch of Lloyd Jack

Henry ap Phillip

Griffith ap Henry of Llanllŷr

Joan m. Hugh Llewellyn Lloyd
3rd son of Castell Hywyl died 1577

Morgan Lloyd m. Elizabeth
died 1604   daughter of
Lewis ap Henry Lloyd
still living 1615

Griffith Lloyd
Principal
Jesus College
Oxford
died 1586

Thomas Lloyd
Chancellor
St David's

Richard Pryse
died 1622

Sir John Pryse   Bridget m. John Lewes
of Gogerddan   of Abernantbychan

Lettice m. Thomas Lloyd
of Llanllŷr

John m. Elin daughter of James Lewes
of Gellydowyll and Abernantbychan

Joan m. James Lewes
of Gellydowyll

Sir Marmaduke Lloyd   Lettice m. Thomas Lewes
of Gernos

Sir Richard Pryse
of Gogerddan

Thomas
(1607-13)

Bridget m. Richard Vaughan
died before   Earl of Carbery
1637

Sir Richard   Sir Thomas Pryse
Pryse of   of Glanfraed
Gogerddan   died 1682

William Lloyd
of Llanllŷr
died 1688

Morgan of
Greengrove

Lettice m. Thomas Lloyd
bought Llanllŷr 1648
died 1649

GENEALOGY

Lewes family circa 1500-1820

Lewes ap David ap Mereudd of Abernanthychan m. Joan daughter of Rhys ap John ap Hywel of Gernos

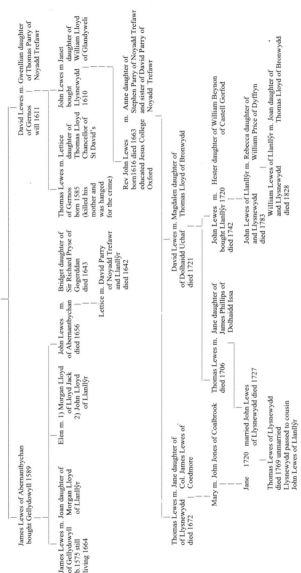

James Lewes of Abernanthychan bought Gellydowyll 1589

David Lewes m. Gwenllian daughter of Gernos of Thomas Parry of will 1611 Noyadd Trefawr

John Lewes m Janet bought daughter of Llysnewydd William Lloyd 1610 of Glandyweli

James Lewes m. Joan daughter of of Gellydowyll Morgan Lloyd b.1575 still of Llanllŷr living 1664

Elen m. 1) Morgan Lloyd of Lloyd Jack 2) John Lloyd of Llanllŷr

John Lewes m. of Abernanthychan died 1656

Bridget daughter of Sir Richard Pryse of Gogerddan died 1643

Thomas Lewes m. Lettice of Gernos daughter of born 1585 Thomas Lloyd (killed his Chancellor of mother and St David's was hanged for the crime)

Anne daughter of Stephen Parry of Noyadd Trefawr and sister of David Parry of Noyadd Trefawr

Lettice m. David Parry of Noyadd Trefawr and Llanllŷr died 1642

Rev John Lewes m. born1616 died 1663 educated Jesus College Oxford

Thomas Lewes m. Jane daughter of of Llysnewydd Col. James Lewes of died 1672 Coedmore

David Lewes m. Magdalen daughter of of Dolhaidd Uchaf Thomas Lloyd of Bronwydd died 1721

John Lewes m. bought Llanllŷr 1720 died 1742

Hester daughter of William Beynon of Castell Gorfod

Mary m. John Jones of Coalbrook

Thomas Lewes m. Jane daughter of died 1706 James Phillips of Dolhaidd Issa

John Lewes of Llanllŷr m. Rebecca daughter of died 1783 William Price of Dyffryn

William Lewes of Llanllŷr m. Joan daughter of and Llysnewydd Thomas Lloyd of Bronwydd died 1828

Jane 1720 married John Lewes of Llysnewydd died 1727

Thomas Lewes of Llysnewydd died 1769 unmarried Llysnewydd passed to cousin John Lewes of Llanllŷr

GENEALOGY

Lewes of Llanllŷr circa 1800-2000

William Lewes of Llysnewydd and Llanllŷr m. Joan daughter of Thomas Lloyd of Bronwydd

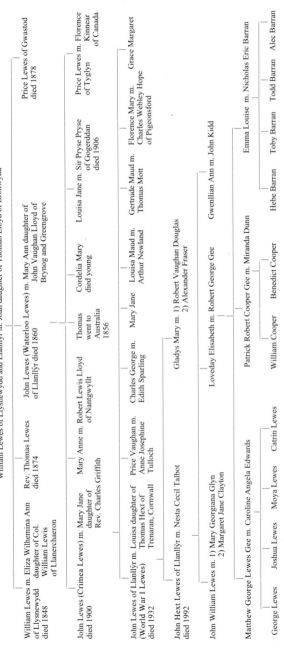

Bibliography

Amherst, Alicia, *A History of Gardening in England*, London, 1896.

Archaeologia Cambrensis, vol. XIII (5th series).

Baring-Gould, S & Fisher, J, *The Lives of the British Saints*, 4 vols, 1907–13.

Bennett, Sue, *Five Centuries of Women and Gardens*, London, 2000.

Bowen, G C, 'The Celtic Saints in Cardiganshire', *Ceredigion* I, 1950, pp.3–17.

Campbell-Culver, Maggie, *The Origin of Plants*, London, 2001.

Cockayne, G E, Gibbs, V et al. (eds), *Complete Peerage*, 14 vols., London, 1910–59.

Daniels, Stephen, *Landscape Gardening and the Geography of Georgian England*, Yale, 1999.

David, Penny, *A Garden Lost in Time*, London, 1999.

Davies, J L & Kirby, D P (eds), *Cardiganshire County History*, Vol.1, Cardiff, 1994.

Davies, Oliver, *Celtic Christianity in Early Medieval Wales*, Cardiff, 1996.

Davies, Wendy, *Wales in the Early Middle Ages*, Leicester, 1982.

Davis, Paul R, & Lloyd-Fern, Susan, *Lost Churches of Wales and the Marches*, Sutton, 1990.

Dineley, Thomas, *The Account of the Official Progress of His Grace Henry the First Duke of Beaufort Through Wales in 1684* (ed. R W Banks) London, 1888.

Edwards, Ifan ap Owen, (ed.), *A Catalogue of Star Chamber Proceedings Relating to Wales*, Cardiff, 1929.

Elkins, Sharon K, *Holy Women of Twelfth Century England*, London, 1988.

Farmer, Hugh David, *The Oxford Dictionary of Saints*, Oxford, 1992 edition.

Fearnley-Whittingstall, Jane, *The Garden: An English Love Affair. One Thousand Years of Gardening*, London, 2003.

Fleming, Lawrence & Gore, Alan, *The English Garden*, London, 1980.

Foster, Joseph, *Alumni Oxonienses 1500–1714*, Vol. Labdon-Ryves, Oxford.

Hadfield, Miles, *A History of British Gardening*, London, 1960.

Jacobus de Voragine, *The Golden Legend: Readings on the Saints*. Translated by Ryan, W R, 2 vols, Princeton, 1993.

Gee, Loveday Lewes, *Women, Art and Patronage: From Henry II to Edward III 1216–1377*. Woodbridge, 2002.

Gilchrist, R, *Contemplation and Action: The Other Monasticism*, London, 1995.

Giraldus Cambrensis Opera, (ed.) Brewer, J S et al, vol.iv, Rolls Series 21, 1873.

Handley, Mark A, 'Isidore of Seville and 'Hisperic Latin' in Early Medieval Wales: The Epigraphic Culture of Llanllŷr and Llanddewi-Brefi', *Roman, Runes and Ogham. Medieval Inscription in the Insular World and on the Continent*, eds Higgitt, John, Forsyth, Katherine and Parsons, David N, Donington, 2001.

Harries, Frederick J, *The Welsh Elizabethans*, Pontypridd, 1924.

Harvey, John, *Medieval Gardens*, 1981.

Hobhouse, Penelope, *Plants in Garden History*, London, 1997.

James, J W, (translator and editor), *Rhygyfarch Vita Davidis: Life of St David*, UWP, 1923.

Jones, Francis, *Historic Cardiganshire Homes and their Families*, Brawdy Books, 2000.

Jones, J Gwynfor, *Wales and the Tudor State*, Cardiff, 1989.

Jones, J Gwynfor, *The Welsh Gentry 1536–1640*, Cardiff, 1998.

Jones, Thomas, (ed.), *Brut y Tywysogion: Chronicle of the Princes*, Cardiff, 1955.

Landsberg, Sylvia, *The Medieval Garden*, British Museum.

Langland, William, *Piers the Plowman*, (translated by J F Goodridge), Penguin, 1966 edition.

Lewes, Evelyn, *Out with the Cambrians*, London, 1934.

Lewes, John Hext, 'Llanllŷr 1180-1980', *Ceredigion* Vol.VI, 1971, pp.341–9.

Lewis, E A, *An Inventory of the Early Chancery Proceedings concerning Wales*, Cardiff, 1937.

Lewis, E A & Conway-Davies, J, *Records of the Court of Augmentations relating to Wales and Monmouthshire*, Cardiff, 1954.

Lloyd, Howell A, *The Gentry of South-West Wales 1540–1640*, Cardiff, 1968.

Lloyd, John Edward, *A History of Wales*, Vol. II, 1912.

Mabey, Richard, (ed.), *The Gardener's Labyrinth* by Thomas Hill, Oxford, 1987.

McLean, Teresa, *Medieval English Gardens*, London, 1981.

O'Hanlon, John, *Lives of the Irish Saints*, Vol. II, Dublin, 1875–1903.

Owen, G Dyfnant, *Elizabethan Wales: The Social Scene*, Cardiff, 1962.

Power, Eileen, *Medieval Women*, London, 1986.

Quest-Ritson, Charles, *The English Garden: A Social History*, London, 2001.

Richards, Charlotte, 'Llanllŷr Before and After the Dissolution of the Monasteries', BA Dissertation, University of Wales Newport, 1999.

Strong, Roy, *The Renaissance Garden in England*, London, 1979.

Suggett, Richard, *John Nash: Architect in Wales*, 1995.

Thomas, Hugh, *A History of Wales 1485–1660*, Cardiff, 1972.

Thompson, Sally, 'Why English Nunneries had no History: A Study of the Problems of the English Nunneries founded after the Conquest', *Distant Echoes: Medieval Religious Women*, Vol. 1, eds Nichols, John A, & Shank, Lillian Thomas, Kalamazoo, 1984.

Toulin-Smith, Lucy, (ed.), *The Itinerary in Wales of John Leland in or about the years 1536–9*, London, 1966.

Turvey, Roger, *The Welsh Princes*, Harlow, 2002.

Uglow, Jenny, *A Little History of British Gardening*, London, 2004.

Victoria County History, Oxfordshire, Vol. 3, London 1954.

Williams, D H, 'Cistercian Nunneries in Wales', *Cîteaux*, 3, 1975.

Williams, D H, *The Welsh Cistercians*, 2001 edition.

Whittle, Elisabeth, *The Historic Gardens of Wales*, London, 1992.

INDEX

Plan & Directions

1 Shrubbery
2 Terrace
3 Shrub Borders
4 Fishpond
5 Rose Garden
6 Water Garden
7 Stage
8 Labyrinth
9 Meridian
10 Laburnum arbour
11 Mound

Llanllŷr, Talsarn, Lampeter, Ceredigion SA48 8QB
☎ 01570 470900
Map ref SN 543559
Six miles north-west of Lampeter on B4337 to Llanrhystud.

The garden opens in June each year in aid of the National Gardens Scheme. Visitors are also welcome by appointment.

Welsh Historic Gardens Trust
Ymddiriedolaeth Gerddi Hanesyddol Cymru

Registered Charity Number 1023293

The gardens, parks and designed landscapes of Wales are an invaluable yet vulnerable part of our heritage. Founded in 1989, the Welsh Historic Gardens Trust is dedicated to the preservation and rescue of historic sites in Wales, from the smallest cottage garden to the largest urban or estate park.

Our aims are to:
- Encourage understanding and appreciation of historic designed landscapes
- Research, record and catalogue gardens and designed landscapes of historic interest
- Campaign for the protection and conservation of sites at risk and advise on their restoration

Members enjoy involvement in Trust activities including:
- An exciting programme of lectures, study days and garden visits organised nationally and by local branches
- Protecting gardens and designed landscapes through research, recording and practical conservation
- Monitoring planning applications and campaigning for the protection of gardens at risk
- Receiving *The Bulletin*, a quarterly newletter with news of activities, events and topical issues, and *Gerddi*, the Trust's biennial journal

If you would like to join the WHGT or want more information about the Trust, please contact The Bothy, Aberglasney, Llangathen, SA32 8QH For information and the latest news, see the WHGT website:
www.whgt.org.uk

For information about the **Ceredigion Branch** of WHGT, please contact Dr Caroline Palmer (Chairman), The Old Laundry, Rhydyfelin, Aberystwyth SY23 4QF